PLAY ON SHAKESPEARE

The Two Gentlemen of Verona

PLAY ON SHAKESPEARE

All's Well That Ends Well	Virginia Grise
Antony and Cleopatra	Christopher Chen
As You Like It	David Ivers
The Comedy of Errors	Christina Anderson
Coriolanus	Sean San José
Cymbeline	Andrea Thome
Edward III	Octavio Solis
Hamlet	Lisa Peterson
Henry IV	Yvette Nolan
Henry V	Lloyd Suh
Henry VI	Douglas P. Langworthy
Henry VIII	Caridad Svich
Julius Caesar	Shishir Kurup
King John	Brighde Mullins
King Lear	Marcus Gardley
Love's Labour's Lost	Josh Wilder
Macbeth	Migdalia Cruz
Measure for Measure	Aditi Brennan Kapil
The Merchant of Venice	Elise Thoron
The Merry Wives of Windsor	Dipika Guha
A Midsummer Night's Dream	Jeffrey Whitty
Much Ado About Nothing	Ranjit Bolt
Othello	Mfoniso Udofia
Pericles	Ellen McLaughlin
Richard II	Naomi Iizuka
Richard III	Migdalia Cruz
Romeo and Juliet	Hansol Jung
The Taming of the Shrew	Amy Freed
The Tempest	Kenneth Cavander
Timon of Athens	Kenneth Cavander
Titus Andronicus	Amy Freed
Troilus and Cressida	Lillian Groag
Twelfth Night	Alison Carey
The Two Gentlemen of Verona	Amelia Roper
The Two Noble Kinsmen	Tim Slover
The Winter's Tale	Tracy Young

The Two Gentlemen of Verona

by
William Shakespeare

Modern verse translation by
Amelia Roper

Dramaturgy by
Kate McConnell

Arizona State University
Tempe, Arizona
2024

———

*Publication of Play On Shakespeare is assisted by
generous support from the Hitz Foundation.
For more information, please visit* www.playonshakespeare.org

———

Published by ACMRS Press
Arizona Center for Medieval and Renaissance Studies,
Arizona State University, Tempe, Arizona
www.acmrspress.com

Library of Congress Cataloging-in-Publication Data
Names: Roper, Amelia, author. | McConnell, Kate, contributor. |
    Shakespeare, William, 1564-1616. Two gentlemen of Verona.
Title: The two gentlemen of Verona / by William Shakespeare ; modern
    verse translation by Amelia Roper ; dramaturgy by Kate McConnell.
Description: Tempe, Arizona : ACMRS Press, 2023. | Series: Play on
    Shakespeare | Summary: "A contemporary translation of one of
    Shakespeare's earliest explorations of love and friendship"-- Provided
    by publisher.
Identifiers: LCCN 2023036752 (print) | LCCN 2023036753 (ebook) |
    ISBN 9780866988292 (paperback) | ISBN 9780866988308 (ebook)
Subjects: LCSH: Triangles (Interpersonal relations)--Drama. | Exiles--
    Drama. | Friendship--Drama. | Verona (Italy)--Drama. | LCGFT:
    Comedy plays.
Classification: LCC PR2878.T9 R67 2023 (print) | LCC PR2878.T9
    (ebook) | DDC 822/.92--dc23/eng/20230804
LC record available at https://lccn.loc.gov/2023036752
LC ebook record available at https://lccn.loc.gov/2023036753

Printed in the United States of America

We wish to acknowledge our gratitude
for the extraordinary generosity of the
Hitz Foundation

～

Special thanks to the Play on Shakespeare staff
Lue Douthit, President and Co-Founder
Taylor Bailey, Producing Director
Cheryl Rizzo, Business Director
Artie Calvert, Finance Director

～

Originally commissioned by the
Oregon Shakespeare Festival
Bill Rauch, Artistic Director
Cynthia Rider, Executive Director

PLAY ON SHAKESPEARE

In 2015, the Oregon Shakespeare Festival announced a new commissioning program. It was called "Play on!: 36 playwrights translate Shakespeare." It elicited a flurry of reactions. For some people this went too far: "You can't touch the language!" For others, it didn't go far enough: "Why not new adaptations?" I figured we would be on the right path if we hit the sweet spot in the middle.

Some of the reaction was due not only to the scale of the project, but its suddenness: 36 playwrights, along with 38 dramaturgs, had been commissioned and assigned to translate 39 plays, and they were already hard at work on the assignment. It also came fully funded by the Hitz Foundation with the shocking sticker price of $3.7 million.

I think most of the negative reaction, however, had to do with the use of the word "translate." It's been difficult to define precisely. It turns out that there is no word for the kind of subtle and rigorous examination of language that we are asking for. We don't mean "word for word," which is what most people think of when they hear the word translate. We don't mean "paraphrase," either.

The project didn't begin with 39 commissions. Linguist John McWhorter's musings about translating Shakespeare is what sparked this project. First published in his 1998 book *Word on the Street* and reprinted in 2010 in *American Theatre* magazine, he notes that the "irony today is that the Russians, the French, and other people in foreign countries possess Shakespeare to a much greater extent than we do, for the simple reason that they get to enjoy Shakespeare in the language they speak."

This intrigued Dave Hitz, a long-time patron of the Oregon Shakespeare Festival, and he offered to support a project that looked at Shakespeare's plays through the lens of the English we speak today. How much has the English language changed since Shakespeare? Is it possible that there are conventions in the early modern English of Shakespeare that don't translate to us today, especially in the moment of hearing it spoken out loud as one does in the theater?

How might we "carry forward" the successful communication between actor and audience that took place 400 years ago? "Carry forward," by the way, is what we mean by "translate." It is the fourth definition of *translate* in the Oxford English Dictionary.

As director of literary development and dramaturgy at the Oregon Shakespeare Festival, I was given the daunting task of figuring out how to administer the project. I began with Kenneth Cavander, who translates ancient Greek tragedies into English. I figured that someone who does that kind of work would lend an air of seriousness to the project. I asked him how might he go about translating from the source language of early modern English into the target language of contemporary modern English?

He looked at different kinds of speech: rhetorical and poetical, soliloquies and crowd scenes, and the puns in comedies. What emerged from his tinkering became a template for the translation commission. These weren't rules exactly, but instructions that every writer was given.

First, do no harm. There is plenty of the language that doesn't need translating. And there is some that does. Every playwright had different criteria for assessing what to change.

Second, go line-by-line. No editing, no cutting, no "fixing." I want the whole play translated. We often cut the gnarly bits in

Shakespeare for performance. What might we make of those bits if we understood them in the moment of hearing them? Might we be less compelled to cut?

Third, all other variables stay the same: the time period, the story, the characters, their motivations, and their thoughts. We designed the experiment to examine the language.

Fourth, and most important, the language must follow the same kind of rigor and pressure as the original, which means honoring the meter, rhyme, rhetoric, image, metaphor, character, action, and theme. Shakespeare's astonishingly compressed language must be respected. Trickiest of all: making sure to work within the structure of the iambic pentameter.

We also didn't know which of Shakespeare's plays might benefit from this kind of investigation: the early comedies, the late tragedies, the highly poetic plays. So we asked three translators who translate plays from other languages into English to examine a Shakespeare play from each genre outlined in the *First Folio*: Kenneth took on *Timon of Athens,* a tragedy; Douglas Langworthy worked on the *Henry the Sixth* history plays, and Ranjit Bolt tried his hand at the comedy *Much Ado about Nothing.*

Kenneth's *Timon* received a production at the Alabama Shakespeare in 2014 and it was on the plane ride home that I thought about expanding the project to include 39 plays. And I wanted to do them all at once. The idea was to capture a snapshot of contemporary modern English. I couldn't oversee that many commissions, and when Ken Hitz (Dave's brother and president of the Hitz Foundation) suggested that we add a dramaturg to each play, the plan suddenly unfolded in front of me. The next day, I made a simple, but extensive, proposal to Dave on how to commission and develop 39 translations in three years. He responded immediately with "Yes."

My initial thought was to only commission translators who translate plays. But I realized that "carry forward" has other meanings. There was a playwright in the middle of the conversation 400 years ago. What would it mean to carry *that* forward?

For one thing, it would mean that we wanted to examine the texts through the lens of performance. I am interested in learning how a dramatist makes sense of the play. Basically, we asked the writers to create performable companion pieces.

I wanted to tease out what we mean by contemporary modern English, and so we created a matrix of writers who embodied many different lived experiences: age, ethnicity, gender-identity, experience with translations, geography, English as a second language, knowledge of Shakespeare, etc.

What the playwrights had in common was a deep love of language and a curiosity about the assignment. Not everyone was on board with the idea and I was eager to see how the experiment would be for them. They also pledged to finish the commission within three years.

To celebrate the completion of the translations, we produced a festival in June 2019 in partnership with The Classic Stage Company in New York to hear all 39 of them. Four hundred years ago I think we went to *hear* a play; today we often go to *see* a play. In the staged reading format of the Festival, we heard these plays as if for the first time. The blend of Shakespeare with another writer was seamless and jarring at the same time. Countless actors and audience members told us that the plays were understandable in ways they had never been before.

Now it's time to share the work. We were thrilled when Ayanna Thompson and her colleagues at the Arizona Center for Medieval and Renaissance Studies offered to publish the translations for us.

I ask that you think of these as marking a moment in time.

The editions published in this series are based on the scripts that were used in the Play on! Festival in 2019. For the purpose of the readings, there were cuts allowed and these scripts represent those reading drafts.

The original commission tasked the playwrights and dramaturg to translate the whole play. The requirement of the commission was for two drafts which is enough to put the ball in play. The real fun with these texts is when there are actors, a director, a dramaturg, and the playwright wrestling with them together in a rehearsal room.

The success of a project of this scale depends on the collaboration and contributions of many people. The playwrights and dramaturgs took the assignment seriously and earnestly and were humble and gracious throughout the development of the translations. Sally Cade Holmes and Holmes Productions, our producer since the beginning, provided a steady and calm influence.

We have worked with more than 1,200 artists in the development of these works. We have partnered with more than three dozen theaters and schools. Numerous readings and more than a dozen productions of these translations have been heard and seen in the United States as well as Canada, England, and the Czech Republic.

There is a saying in the theater that 80% of the director's job is taken care of when the production is cast well. Such was my luck when I hired Taylor Bailey, who has overseen every reading and workshop, and was the producer of the Festival in New York. Katie Kennedy has gathered all the essays, and we have been supported by the rest of the Play on Shakespeare team: Kamilah Long, Summer Martin, and Amrita Ramanan.

All of this has come to be because Bill Rauch, then artistic director of the Oregon Shakespeare Festival, said yes when Dave

Hitz pitched the idea to him in 2011. Actually he said, "Hmm, interesting," which I translated to "yes." I am dearly indebted to that 'yes.'

My gratitude to Dave, Ken, and the Hitz Foundation can never be fully expressed. Their generosity, patience, and unwavering belief in what we are doing has given us the confidence to follow the advice of Samuel Beckett: "Ever tried. Ever failed. No matter. Try again. Fail again. Fail better."

Play on!

Dr. Lue Douthit
CEO/Creative Director at Play on Shakespeare
October 2020

WHAT WAS I THINKING?
Kate McConnell

I AM THE ELDEST BOY!

Two Gentleman of Verona was a young play for Shakespeare, written in the late 1580s or early 1590s and believed by many to be his first. The tropes and techniques he began to experiment with here as a young writer would be developed much more fully and successfully in his later plays such as *Romeo and Juliet*, *As You Like It*, and *Twelfth Night*.

It is also oft forgotten that the characters of Valentine and Proteus (like so many of Shakespeare's characters) are themselves very young too. They may be expected to marry and take power at a ridiculously young age but these men are teens. They talk about girls at length, but have likely never touched one. They talk of the world and their important place in it, but are both at the mercy of parental whims. They are fiercely impatient, excitable but also neurotic, afraid, insecure, impulsive, and entitled. They are the original Kendall Roys! And there is much fun to be had in the manic energy of this play, if one knows where to look.

This overall concept of youth gave Amelia a clear way into the text, exploring the larger themes of fear, hope, and injustice through impulsive adolescence. The abrupt shift from friendship to competition between the boys as well as the objectification and even crudity in their relationships with women and servants sits in what is actually a love story structure … if the lovers were Valentine and Proteus. Their platonic friendship provides the biggest stakes, heartbreaks, and happy endings. Julia and Sylvia may be vastly more intelligent, articulate, and sensible, but are treated as toys. Bros before hoes all the way!

In one of the most disturbing happy endings of all Shake-speare's plays, Valentine "gives" Sylvia to Proteus. And Proteus sees no problem with taking her, consent or no. Sylvia herself gets no lines, and never speaks again. While the task for all Play On!'s play-wrights was clear (they were to translate the plays, not "fix" them), Amelia was passionate about highlighting the toxic masculinity, not ignoring it. After all, the plight of women is a theme Shake-speare returns to again and again, though arguably he finds a better way to give these gorgeous women voices by the time he is writing, say, *Richard III*.

Another way youth was realized in Amelia's text was through vulgar language. It may be important to note here that Amelia Roper is Australian. She is also a comedy writer for TV and film, most notably HULU's *The Great*. We quickly discovered that pro-fanity of all styles came easily and casually to her, just as (she felt strongly) it does to boys like this. So we began the detailed work of deciding which politely cheeky Elizabethan words to translate, and what to change it to. It was a lively discussion between us, the actors, and some rather distraught audience members at the Play On! Festival in 2019.

In the end, Amelia simply deployed the expletives that she felt best fit the meaning, mood, and energy of a line. Which is the entire point of the project after all. And just as Shakespeare wrote to be performed and not read, rhythm and rhyme is key for Amelia, as is the politics of this play, in particular themes of power, corrup-tion, class, and gender. If one wants to be angry at the "f word" she says, let that word be "fairness" and the sad lack of it in all iterations of this play and this world, new and old. Oh and hey, it's a comedy. Enjoy.

CHARACTERS IN THE PLAY
(in order of speaking)

VALENTINE, Socialite teenager with a trust fund. Think #richkidsofinstagram

PROTEUS, Valentine's closest friend. Socialite teenager with a trust fund

SPEED, Valentine's Personal Assistant

JULIA, Socialite teenager with a trust fund

LUCETTA, Julia's Personal Assistant

ANTONIO, Proteus's father

PANTINO, Antonio's Intern

SYLVIA, Socialite teenager with a trust fund in Milan

LANCE, Proteus's Personal Assistant

CRAB, Lance's dog

THURIO, Valentine's rival for Silvia

DUKE OF MILAN, Silvia's father

O'ONE, an outlaw

O'TWO, an outlaw

O'THREE, an outlaw

HOTELIER, host of the hotel in Milan

EGLAMORE, family friend of the Duke

Other Interns, Musicians, and Outlaws

ACT 1 ◆ SCENE 1

Enter Valentine and Proteus

VALENTINE

Stop protesting, my loving Proteus,
Yokel kids, have ever vocal wits,
Were it not that your sticky Love,
Keeps you stuck here,
I would demand you join me,   5
To see the wonders of the world outside,
Than, snoozing and losing at home,
Squander your youth with idleness!
But, thou lovest. Love still, and shine inside,
As I will, ugh, when 'tis I find some shiny bride.   10

PROTEUS

Will you be gone? Sweet Valentine goodbye!
Think on your Bro-teus, when you fall upon
Some fallen object in your travels. (*clearly talking about a woman*)
Wish me share in your triumph,
When you do meet good (*sex action*) umph! And in your danger, 15
If ever danger do threaten you,
Announce your grievance to my holy prayers,
For I will be your monk, Valentine.

VALENTINE

And on a Love book pray for my success?

PROTEUS

Upon some book I Love, I'll pray for thee.   20

VALENTINE (*mildly impressed*)

That's some small story of big Love,
How young Romeo died for Juliet.

1

PROTEUS (*less impressed*)
   More like a big story of a small Love,
   For he was over-shoes in Love with two!
VALENTINE
   It's true, you are over-shoes in Love with one,   25
   And yet you are afraid of jumping.
PROTEUS
   What?
VALENTINE
   It suit you not.
   To be in Love! To hope a "no!" means "yes",
   Coy looks, heart breaking sighs. For every fleeting touch,   30
   Twenty sick, watchful, weary, tedious nights,
   If simply won, perhaps a (*points to head*) simple gain,
   If lost, why then an epic battle won,
   Either way, you're fucked.
PROTEUS
   You call me fucked!   35
VALENTINE
   Fucking is all you think about.
PROTEUS
   'Tis Love you tease, I am not Love.
VALENTINE
   Yeah, well I'm off. My Father waits,
   He's walking me to the bus. (*embarrassed*) He insisted.
PROTEUS
   Great! I will walk you too, Valentine!   40
VALENTINE
   Sweet Proteus, no. Now let's say goodbye.
   Write to me. Let me hear everything.
   All your battles in Love, and whatever else
   Goes down here in absence of your Friend,

And I likewise will write you mine.   45

They hug, awkward man hug

PROTEUS

All happiness happen to you in Millan.

VALENTINE

As much to you at home, and so farewell.

Exit Valentine

PROTEUS

He after Honor hunts, I after Love,

He leaves his friends to dignify them more,

I leave myself, my friends, and all for Love.   50

Cruel Julia, you have metamorphosed me!

Made me neglect my Studies, waste my time,

Fight with good advice, reject the outside world,

Made my head hurt, heart hurt, heart sick with thought.

Enter Speed

SPEED

Fuck! Hi. Have you seen gentle Valentine?   55

PROTEUS

Gone! Lost! A distant memory! *(Speed is shocked, dead?)* He's

on the bus.

SPEED

Agh! I have missed the bus, lost my bus ticket,

And lost my boss. I am a baaaaad sheep!

PROTEUS

Yep.   60

SPEED

You agree that Valentine is a shepherd, and I, a sheep?

PROTEUS

I do.

SPEED

Yet I will follow him, *(singing)* follow him, follow him,

wherever he! may go!

PROTEUS

Just ... one more thing. Did you give my Letter to Julia? 65

SPEED

Yes Sir. I, a little lamb, gave your Letter to her, a fairy tale Mary, and her, a fairy tale Mary, gave me nothing for my troubles.

PROTEUS

Troubles? Why, what did she say?

> *Speed nods furiously, shakes his head furiously,*
> *nods, shakes, and shrugs*

PROTEUS

Women! 70

SPEED

You mistake me, Sir. She said something sensible, I just did not understand it.

(*shrugs again*) Big words.

PROTEUS

But she has the letter?

SPEED

Yes. And ... 75

PROTEUS

And, and, and, and what?!

SPEED

Hmm. I may remember more, with more.

PROTEUS (*giving money*)

Here is for your troubles. What did she say? Fuck!

SPEED (*looking at the money*)

Honestly, nope, I don't think you'll win her.

PROTEUS

Why? What did she say!! 80

SPEED

Unclear. Very confusing. But pretty.

Exit Speed

PROTEUS

Go! Go, be gone, the bus is slow and stupid, you'll love it.

I'll write again. And again! And again!

And again God damn it, she will love me!

(*writes*)

Kind Julia …   85

One of a kind Julia?

Yo. Julia.

Exit Proteus

ACT 1 ◆ SCENE 2

Enter Julia and Lucetta

JULIA

Of all the guys, hundreds of guys

That visit every day, and write, and sing at me,

Which, in your opinion, is most gentlemanly?

LUCETTA

If you repeat their names, I'll show my mind,

According to my shallow simple skill.   5

JULIA

What do you think of the fair Sir Eglamore?

LUCETTA

As of a Knight, well-spoken, neat, and fine.

But if I were you, he would never be mine.

JULIA

What do you think of the rich Mercatio?

LUCETTA

Of his wealth, yes please, but of himself, so, so.   10

JULIA

What do you think of … gentle Proteus?

LUCETTA

Hell no. No. No way. Proteus? *Gentle*?

JULIA

He's okay. Or … not? What is this passion at his name?

LUCETTA

Sorry dear Julia, it's silly really

That I, me, a nobody as I am,   15

Should speak out against lovely Gentlemen.

JULIA

Why passion for Proteus, why not the rest?

LUCETTA

If you think him good, then I think him best.

JULIA

Your reason?

LUCETTA

I have no other but a woman's reason,   20

I think him so because I think him so.

JULIA

I wish I knew his mind.

LUCETTA

Enjoy this letter Madam. (*handing her a letter*)

JULIA (*reads*)

"To Julia …" For me! From who?

LUCETTA

Oh, it'll be obvious.   25

JULIA

But who delivered it?

LUCETTA

Sir Valentine's page, Speed. Sent from gentleman Proteus.

I took it in your name. Hope that's okay.

JULIA

  Now by my modesty, a goodly savior!

  Do you hope to protect me from disgrace?   30

  To whisper and conspire against my innocence?

  Now trust me, it's a job of great importance,

  And you an officer fit for the place!

  There. Take the paper. See it be returned,

  Or else return no more into my sight!   35

LUCETTA (*taking the paper*)

  To plead for Love, deserves more cash, than hate.

JULIA

  Will you be gone?

LUCETTA

  That you may ruminate.

Exit Lucetta

JULIA

  And yet I should have peeked at the Letter.

  So embarrassing to call her back again,   40

  And pray she let me see when I teased her.

  What fool is she, she knows I am a Maid,

  And would not force the letter to my face?

  Since Maids, in modesty, say "no", to that,

  Which they would rather say "hell yes!"   45

  Shit, shit. How fickle is this foolish Love.

  That like a testy babe will scratch the Nurse,

  And presently, all humbled kiss her cheek?

  How childishly, I tease Lucetta hence,

  When willingly, I would have had her here?   50

  How angrily I taught my brow to frown,

  When inward joy forced my heart to smile?

  My penance is, to call Lucetta back

  And ask forgiveness, for my stupid past.

Hey, hi, hello, Lucetta!   55

Enter Lucetta

LUCETTA

What would your Ladyship?

JULIA

Is't near dinner time?

LUCETTA

I wish it were,

That you might fight your meat and not your Maid.

Lucetta drops the paper. Picks it up.

JULIA

What is't that you took up so gingerly?   60

LUCETTA

Nothing.

JULIA

Why did you stoop then?

LUCETTA

To take up a paper, that I let fall.

JULIA

And is that paper nothing?

LUCETTA

None of my business.   65

JULIA

Then let it lie! For we are too busy.

Julia is not busy. Eventually …

JULIA

Some Love of yours has sent you a rhyme.

LUCETTA

Name a tune, your ladyship, I'll sing it.

JULIA

Best sing it to the tune of Light O, Love!

LUCETTA

It is too heavy for so light a tune. 70

JULIA

Heavy? Has it some tragedy? Some news?

LUCETTA

Only news if you sing it,

JULIA

And why not you?

LUCETTA

I cannot reach so high.

JULIA (*taking the paper*)

Let's see your Song, Lucetta. What's this? 75

LUCETTA

Keep tune there still, so you will sing it out.

And yet I think I do not like this tune.

JULIA

You do not?

LUCETTA

No, Madam, far too sharp.

JULIA

You, dear friend, are too saucy! 80

LUCETTA

Nay, now you are too flat.

And twang the harmony, with too harsh a discord.

There wanting but a bongo to fill your Song.

JULIA

The bongo is drowned with your unruly dancing!

Enough of this babble. Trouble me no more. 85

Here is my answer to his sad efforts, I protest even the

happy attempt!

Julia rips up the paper.

Lucetta begins to pick up the pieces.

Go! Get you gone. And let the papers lie.
You would be fingering them to anger me.

LUCETTA

She acts strange, but I think she'd be much pleased,
To be so angered with another Letter.   90

Exit Lucetta

JULIA

Shit, shit, shit, fuck, shit! I hope he sends another!
Oh hateful hands, to break such loving words!
I'll kiss each piece of paper, for amends.

(*picking up the pieces*)

Look, here it says "kind Julia." Unkind Julia!
As in revenge of my ingratitude,   95
I throw my name against the bruising stones,
Trampling contemptuously on my disdain.
And here it says, "Love wounded Proteus."
Poor wounded name! My bosom, as a bed,
Shall hold you till your pain be thoroughly healed.   100
And so I wake you with a magic kiss.
But twice, or thrice, was "Proteus" written down.
Be calm, good wind. Blow not a word away,
Till I have found each letter, in the Letter.
p a s s i o n a t e   105
Passionate! Passionate ... Proteus,
"To the sweet Julia." That I'll tear away.
And yet I will not, see how lovingly
He couples it with his own sweet, sweet name!
Thus will I fold them one upon another.   110
Now kiss sweetly, embrace, do what you will.

Enter Lucetta

LUCETTA

Madam. Dinner is ready. And your Father waits.

JULIA

Fine!

LUCETTA

What, shall these papers lie, like telltales here?

JULIA

If you care for them, best clean them up.   115

LUCETTA

No way, I was cleaned up, for laying them down.

Yet here they shall not lie, for catching cold.

Lucetta picks up the rest of the pieces

JULIA

I see you have a great desire for them.

LUCETTA

Yes, Madam, you may say what sights you see,

I see things too, I do. You think, I wink.   120

JULIA

Come, come, will you go! Please!

Exit

ACT 1 ◆ SCENE 3

Enter Antonio and Pantino, whispering to others

ANTONIO

Tell me Pantino, what sad talk is this?

My brother whispers, laughs, shakes his head at me?

PANTINO

Not at you, at the young Proteus, your Son.

ANTONIO

Why? What of him?

PANTINO

He wondered that your Lordship   5

Would allow him to spend his youth at home,

While other men, of smaller reputation

11

Put forth their sons, to seek adventure out.
Some to the wars, to try their fortune there.
Some, to discover islands far away. 10
Some, to the studious universities.
For any, or for all these exercises,
He said, that Proteus, your son, was ready.
And did request me mention, well, suggest
You let him spend his time no more at home, 15
Which would be a tragic waste to his age,
In having known no travel in his youth.

ANTONIO

A good idea, and one I've had already,
Though my brother will enjoy his influence.
Yes, I have considered my son's future, 20
And how he'll never be a perfect man
Without adventure, learning, and … adventure.
Experience is by … experience achieved.
And achievement is for the young and brave.
So … tell me, where do I best send him? 25

PANTINO

I think your Lordship knows youthful Valentine.

ANTONIO

I know him well.

PANTINO

Valentine attends the Grand Duke in his Royal Court.
Might be good, I think, if you send your son?
There shall he practice jousting and football. 30
Hear sweet discourse, converse with noblemen,
Be in the thick of every exercise
Worthy his youth, and nobleness of birth.

ANTONIO

Yes. Good chats. You have advised me well.

I like it so much I'll do it today.　　　　　　　　　35

As I would have done anyway,

PANTINO

Of course.

ANTONIO

Now with the speediest expedition,

I will dispatch him to the Grand Duke's Court.

PANTINO

Tomorrow, may it please you, Don Alphonso,　　40

And some Gentlemen I know from football

Are traveling to the Grand Duke's palace,

You could send your young son along with them.

ANTONIO

Good company! Proteus shall join them.

Enter Proteus, reading

Perfect timing! Tell him! Wait, I'll tell him.　　45

PROTEUS (*to himself*)

Sweet Love, sweet lines, sweet life!

Here is her hand, the agent of her heart.

Here is her oath for Love, her great promise.

Oh that our Fathers would applaud our loves

And seal our happiness with their consents!　　50

Oh heavenly Julia!

ANTONIO

How now? What Letter are you reading there?

PROTEUS

May it please your Lordship, it is a word or two

Of ridiculous tales from Valentine.

Delivered ah, by a horse, that rode by.　　55

ANTONIO

Lend me the Letter. Let me see what news.

PROTEUS

    There is no news, my Lord. He writes rhymes of

    How happily he lives, how well beloved,

    And daily graced by the Grand Duke.

    Wishing me with him, to enjoy his fun.   60

ANTONIO

    And how do you feel about your friend's wish?

PROTEUS

    How do *you* feel about it? Not up to me,

    If only I could act on friendly wishes …

ANTONIO

    My will is something friendly, like his wish.

    Wonder not what I imagine for you,   65

    For what I will, I will, and there an end.

    I've decided that you must spend some time

    With Valentine, in the Emperor's Court.

    What money he from his family receives,

    I'll double it, and you shall go happy.   70

    Be up early tomorrow, well dressed, packed,

    And excuse it not. For I am absolute.

PROTEUS

    My Lord! I cannot pack my shoes so soon,

    Please give me a day or two, or eleven?

ANTONIO

    Whatever you forget, your mom will send   75

(*Proteus protests*)

    No more of this, tomorrow you must go!

                     Exit Antonio and Pantino

PROTEUS

    Thus have I jumped the fire for fear of burning

    And fallen in the sea, where I am drowned!

    I feared to show my Father Julia's letter,

Lest he should take exception to my Love,   80
And with the help of my own excuse
Has he most fucked up my Love!
Oh, how this spring of Love resembles
The uncertain glory of an April day,
Which now shows all the beauty of the Sun,   85
And by and by a cloud takes all away.

Enter Pantino

PANTINO

Sir Proteus, your Father calls for you.
He is in haste, therefore I pray you go.

PROTEUS

Why this it is! My heart agrees thereto,
(*aside*) And yet a thousand times it answers "no!"   90

Exit

ACT 2 ◆ SCENE 1

Enter Valentine and Speed

VALENTINE

Ah, Sylvia, Sylvia!

SPEED

Madam Sylvia! Madam Sylvia!

VALENTINE

How now servant?

SPEED

She is not within hearing, Sir.

VALENTINE

Why sir, who asked you to call her? 5

SPEED

Your worship sir, or else I mistook.

VALENTINE

Well, you'll still be too forward.

SPEED

And yet I was last slapped for being too slow.

VALENTINE

Go to, sir, tell me, do you know Madam Sylvia?

SPEED

She that your worship loves? 10

VALENTINE

Why! How do you know that I am in Love?

SPEED

Well, a few things. Let's see. First, you have learned, like Sir
Proteus, to fold your arms like a grump, to hum a Love song
like a bird, to walk alone like one that had the plague, to
weep, like a schoolboy who has buried his Granny. The old 15

17

Valentine walked like a lion, ate like a lion, laughed like a … a

VALENTINE

Lion! Haha!

SPEED

Now when I look on you, I can hardly think you my master.

VALENTINE

Well I am!

SPEED

Yep.   20

VALENTINE

I am your master … and your lion!

SPEED

And I am your sheep.

VALENTINE

Yes! I think so. What does that mean? Doesn't matter, tell me,
do you know my Lady Sylvia?

SPEED

She that you gaze on, as she sits at supper?   25

VALENTINE

Have you noticed that? Or seen her at all?

SPEED

Why sir, I know her not.

VALENTINE

You know I gaze on her, yet know her not?

SPEED

What does she look like?

VALENTINE

Her beauty is beautiful, her qualities, quality.   30

SPEED

Oh.

VALENTINE

"Oh" what?

SPEED

You haven't seen her since she was deformed.

VALENTINE

How long has she been deformed?

SPEED

Ever since you Loved her.   35

VALENTINE

I have Loved her ever since I saw her,

And still I see her beautiful.

SPEED

If you Love her, you cannot see her.

VALENTINE

Why?

SPEED

Because Love is blind! Oh that you had my eyes, or the eyes   40
you had before the lights went out.

VALENTINE

What should I see then?

SPEED

Your folly, and her deformity. For Sir Proteus, being in Love,
could not see to pull up his pants. And you, being in Love,
cannot see to put on your pants.   45

VALENTINE

Then you are in Love, gentle employee!

For today you couldn't see to clean my shoes!

SPEED

True, sir, I was in Love with my bed. I thank you, you slapped
me for my Love, which makes me the bolder to tease you for
yours.   50

VALENTINE

Hmm. Well in conclusion, I Love her.

SPEED

Yep.

VALENTINE

Last night she asked me to compose some lines to one she loves.

SPEED

And have you?

VALENTINE

I have. 55

SPEED

Did you write them badly?

VALENTINE

No! They are brilliant, I think, sort of. Shh! Here she comes.

Enter Sylvia

SPEED (*aside*)

Now he will dance for her. Oh excellent spectacle, oh fun Puppet.

VALENTINE

Madam and Mistress, a thousand good mornings. 60

SPEED (*aside*)

Oh, hello, goodbye, please, thank you, a million manners.

SYLVIA

Sir Valentine, and employee, to you a thousand good days.

SPEED (*aside*)

He invests wisely and gets a good return.

VALENTINE

As you employed me I have penned you a letter,

To the secret, nameless Friend of yours. 65

Which I was much unwilling to proceed in,

But for my duty to your Ladyship.

Valentine gives Sylvia the paper

SYLVIA

I thank you, gentle servant.

(*she reads*)

'Tis very Clerkly done

VALENTINE

Now trust me, Madam, it wasn't easy. 70

I rhymed at random, very ignorantly,

Blind as I am to who I will seduce.

SYLVIA

Do you feel the favor is beneath you?

VALENTINE

No, Madam, so it pleases you, I'll write.

Your friendship inspires a thousand more rhymes, 75

And yet,

SYLVIA

A pretty period. Well. I guess the sequel,

And yet I will not name it, and yet I care not.

And yet, take this again,

(*holding out the paper*)

And yet I thank you. 80

I will trouble you no more.

SPEED (*aside*)

And yet you will, and yet, another yet!

VALENTINE

What means your Ladyship? Do you not like it?

SYLVIA

Yes, yes. The lines are very quaintly written.

But since unwillingly, take them again. 85

(*again, holding out the paper*)

No, take them.

VALENTINE

Madam, they are for you.

SYLVIA

Yes, yes, you chose them Sir, at my request,

But I will none of them. They are for you.

I would have designed them more passionately,   90

VALENTINE (*taking the paper*)

Please you! I'll write your ladyship another.

SYLVIA

And when it's done, for my sake read it over,

And if it please you, great. And if not, why so.

VALENTINE

If it please me, madam? What then?

SYLVIA

Why if it please you, take it for your small fee.   95

And so good day, employee.

Exit Sylvia

SPEED (*aside*)

Oh yes! Unpredictable! Inscrutable! Invisible!

As a nose on a man's face, or a cross on a church,

My master pursues her, and she has taught her suitor,

He being her pupil, to become her tutor.   100

Oh excellent disguise, was there ever heard a better?

That my master being poet, to himself, should write the letter!

VALENTINE

How now Sir? What are you reasoning with yourself?

SPEED

No, I was rhyming, 'tis you have the reason.

VALENTINE

To do what?   105

SPEED

To be a spokesman from Madam Sylvia!

VALENTINE

To who?

SPEED

To yourself! Why, she woos you artfully.

VALENTINE

What art?

SPEED

By a letter, I should say.   110

VALENTINE

Why? She has not written to me!

SPEED

What need she,

When she has made you write to yourself?

Why, do you not perceive the jest?

VALENTINE

No, believe me.   115

SPEED

No believing you indeed sir.

But did you understand her message?

VALENTINE

She gave me none! Except an angry word.

SPEED

Why she hath given you a letter.

VALENTINE

That's the letter I wrote to her Friend!   120

SPEED

And the letter hath she delivered. The End!

VALENTINE

Can it get any worse!

SPEED

Listen to me, it's perfect,

For often have you written her, and she in modesty,

Or else for want of idle time, could not again reply,   125

Or fearing else some messenger, that might her mind discover,

Herself has taught her Love himself! To write unto her lover!

All this I speak in print, for in print I found it.

23   ·

Why worry you sir, 'tis dinner time.

VALENTINE

I have eaten. 130

SPEED

Uh huh, but come on! Your magical Love

Can feed on the air, I need my meat.

Oh, be not like your mistress, be moved, be moved!

Exit

ACT 2 ◆ SCENE 2

Enter Proteus and Julia

PROTEUS

Have patience, gentle Julia.

JULIA

Oh be patient I will! Since there is no other remedy.

PROTEUS

I'll go and when I can, I will return.

JULIA

If you don't go, you will return sooner.

(*giving him a ring*)

Keep this remembrance for your Julia's sake. 5

PROTEUS

Why then we'll make exchange.

(*giving her his ring*)

Here, take you this.

JULIA

And seal the bargain with an honest kiss.

PROTEUS

Here is my hand, for my dedication.

And when that hour over comes me in the day 10

Wherein I sigh not Julia for thy sake,

The next ensuing hour, some foul pain

24

Torment me for my love's forgetfulness!
My Father waits for me. Say nothing!
The tide is high, no, not your tide of tears,   15
That tide will stay me longer than I should,
Julia, farewell!

Exit Julia

What? Gone without a word?

Enter Pantino

PANTINO

Sir Proteus, you are called for.

PROTEUS

Go! I come, I come!   20
Alas, this parting strikes poor lovers dumb.

Exit

ACT 2 ◆ SCENE 3

Enter Lance, weeping, and Crab

LANCE

I'll stop. I've stopped. (*still crying*) Oh God! What weakness!
I have received my orders, like the prodigious son, and I'm
going with Sir Proteus to the Duke's Court. I think Crab, my
dog, be the meanest natured dog that lives! My Mother weeping. My Father wailing. My Sister crying, our Maid howling.   5
Our cat wringing her hands, and all our house in a great
shock and horror, yet did not this cruel hearted jerk shed
one tear. He is a stone, a marble, and has no more pity in him
than a dog. A murderer would have wept to have seen our
parting. Why my granny having no eyes, look you, wept her- 10
self blind at my goodbye! Nay, I'll show you the manner of it.
(*taking off his right shoe*)
This shoe is my Father.
No, this left shoe is my Father. No, no, this left shoe is my

mother. No, that cannot be so neither.

(*taking off his left shoe*)

Yes. It is so, it is so. It has the worser sole! This shoe with   15
the hole in it, is my mother. And this my Father. Hmm. This
umbrella is my sister. For, look you, she is as bright as a lily,
and as small as a wand. This hat is Nan, our maid. I am the
dog. No! The dog is himself, and I am the dog. Oh the dog
is me and I am myself! Yes, so, so, now come I to my Father.   20
"Father, your blessing." Now should not the shoe speak a
word for weeping! Now should I kiss my Father.

(*he kisses his shoe*)

Well, he weeps on. Now come I to my Mother. Oh, that she
could speak now, like a good woman. Well, I kiss her.

(*kissing his other shoe*)

Why there 'tis, here's my mother's breath oh yes indeed. Now   25
come I to my sister, hear the moan she makes! Now the dog
all this while sheds not a tear! Nor speaks a word! But see
how I lay the dust with my tears!

Enter Pantino

PANTINO

Lance! Away, away! Master Proteus is shipped! Go or you'll
swim after him with flippers! What's the matter? Why weep   30
man? Away idiot! You'll lose him if you wait much longer.

LANCE

I go. Ah, bus or boat?

PANTINO

Boat! Swim! Flippers! Ah, the tide is high.

LANCE

It is the unkindest high tide, that ever a man tied!

PANTINO

What's the unkindest high tide?   35

LANCE

Why, he's tied here, Crab, my dog.

CRAB

Hi.

PANTINO

You idiot! I mean you'll lose the flood, and in losing the flood, lose your voyage, and in losing your voyage, lose your Master, and in losing your Master, lose your service, and in 40 losing your service …

LANCE

Lose the tide, and the voyage, and the master, and my service! Why man, if the ocean were dry, I'll be able to fill it with my tears. If the wind were down, I could fill sails with my sighs.

PANTINO

Please go, they sent me to call you. 45

LANCE

Sir, call me whatever you like.

PANTINO

Will you go?

LANCE

Well, okay okay, I will go.

Exit

ACT 2 ◆ SCENE 4

Enter Valentine, Sylvia, Thurio, and Speed

SYLVIA

Employee!

VALENTINE

Mistress.

SPEED

Master, Sir Thurio frowns on you.

VALENTINE
 Yes friend, it's for Love.
SPEED
 Not of you.   5
VALENTINE
 Of my mistress then.
SPEED
 It was good you punched him.
SYLVIA
 Gentle Sir, you are sad.
VALENTINE
 Indeed, Madam, I seem so.
THURIO
 Seem you that you are not?   10
VALENTINE
 Happily I do.
THURIO
 So do fakes, you, faker!
VALENTINE
 So do you.
THURIO
 What do I fake? What am I not?
VALENTINE
 Wise.   15
THURIO
 What proof?
VALENTINE
 Your folly.
THURIO
 And how do you know my folly?
VALENTINE
 I know it in your jacket.

THURIO

  My jacket is a doublet.   20

VALENTINE

  Well then, you double your folly.

SYLVIA

  No more, gentlemen, no more. Here comes my Father.

DUKE

  Now, daughter Sylvia, you are popular.

  Sir Valentine, your Father is in good health,

  And do you miss your friends? Would you like news?   25

VALENTINE

  My Lord, I am always thankful,

  For any message from home.

DUKE

  Know you Don Antonio, your countryman?

VALENTINE

  Aye, my good Lord, I know the gentleman

  To be of good standing, righteous, and popular,   30

  He has capital and a capital reputation.

DUKE

  Has he not a son?

VALENTINE

  Yes, my good Lord, a son, that well deserves

  The Honor, and regard of such a capital Father.

DUKE

  You know him well?   35

VALENTINE

  I knew him as myself. For from our infancy

  We have messed about and spent our hours together.

  And while myself have been an idle truant,

  Enjoying the sweet benefit of time

  To fill my days with fun shenanigans,   40

Yet has Sir Proteus, for that's his name,
Made use, and fair advantage of his days.
His years are young, but his experience old.
His head fierce, but his judgement right.
And in a word, though he is worth far more   45
Than the few praises I now bestow,
He is complete in feature, and in mind,
With all good grace, to grace a Gentleman.

DUKE
Indeed, sir, this Gentleman is come to me
With Commendation from impressive friends,   50
And here he means to spend his time awhile.
I think it's welcome news to you?

VALENTINE
Should I have wished a thing, it had been he!

DUKE
Welcome him then, according to his worth.
Sylvia, I speak to you, and you Sir Thurio,   55
For Valentine needs no introduction,
I'll find him and send him your way. Behave.

Exit Duke

VALENTINE
This is the Gentleman I told your Ladyship
Would have come along with me, but his Love
Held his eyes in hers, together, forever.   60

SYLVIA
Sounds like she is free at last.

VALENTINE
I think she holds him prisoner still.

SYLVIA
Well then he should be blind, and being blind
How could he see his way to look for you?

VALENTINE

Why lady, Love has twenty pairs of eyes.   65

THURIO

They say that Love hath no eyes at all.

VALENTINE

Love winks at all. Even you, Thurio.

One day, Sir, someone, somewhere, will see you.

SYLVIA

Enough, enough. Here comes the gentleman.

Enter Proteus, charming

Exit Thurio, annoyed

VALENTINE

Welcome, dear Proteus! Mistress, I pray to you   70

Celebrate his welcome, with some special favor.

SYLVIA

Your rambling is his guarantee of welcome here,

If this be he you so often wish'd to hear from.

VALENTINE

Mistress, it is. Sweet lady, entertain him

To be my fellow servant to your Ladyship.   75

SYLVIA

Too imperfect a mistress for so perfect a servant.

PROTEUS

Not so, sweet lady, too innocent a servant,

For so entertaining a mistress.

VALENTINE

Give up the humble boy.

Sweet lady, please, find him employment.   80

PROTEUS

My duty will I boast of, nothing else.

SYLVIA

And never did I want less duty, more boasting.

Servant, you are welcome to a worthless mistress.

PROTEUS

I'll die on him that says so but yourself.

SYLVIA

That you are welcome? 85

PROTEUS

That you are worthless.

Enter Thurio

THURIO

Madam, my Lord, your Father would speak with you.

SYLVIA

I wait upon his pleasure.

Come Sir Thurio,

Go with me. Once more new servant, welcome. 90

I'll leave you country girls to gossip.

When you have done, find us.

PROTEUS

We will. Both. Your ladyship.

Exit Sylvia and Thurio

VALENTINE

Now tell me all the news from home!

PROTEUS

Your friends are well, and spoken well of you. 95

VALENTINE

And how do yours?

PROTEUS

I left them all in health.

VALENTINE

How does your lady? And how goes your Love?

PROTEUS

My tales of Love did enrage you once,

I know you don't enjoy them, gentle friend. 100

VALENTINE

    Ah Proteus, but that life is altered now,

    I have done penance for condemning Love,

    Love, Love, glorious Love has punished me

    With upset stomach, with regretful cries,

    With nightly tears, and daily, heart-sore sighs,   105

    For in revenge of my contempt of Love,

    Love hath chased sleep from my addicted eyes,

    And made them watchers of mine own heart's sorrow.

    O gentle Proteus, Love's a mighty Lord,

    And hath so humbled me, as I confess   110

    There is no woe to his correction!

    Nor to his duty, no such joy on earth.

    Now, no other story, except it be of Love.

    Now can I break my fast, dine, drink, and sleep,

    Upon the very naked name of Love!   115

PROTEUS

    Enough. I read your fortune in your eye.

    Was this the idol that you worship so?

VALENTINE

    Yes she! Is she not a heavenly Saint?

PROTEUS

    No. But she is a nice person.

VALENTINE

    Call her divine.   120

PROTEUS

    I will not flatter her.

VALENTINE

    O flatter me! For Love delights in praises.

PROTEUS

    When I was sick, you gave me bitter pills,

    I must revenge my suffering.

VALENTINE

    Then speak the truth by her, if not divine,   125

    Yet let her be a principality,

    Supreme to all the Creatures on the earth.

PROTEUS

    All except my mistress.

VALENTINE

    Cute. Except no, not any,

    Except you will accept my brighter Love.   130

PROTEUS

    Have I not reason to prefer my own?

VALENTINE

    And I will help you to prefer her too,

    She will be dignified with the highest Honor,

    To carry my lady's shopping.

    For my lady deserves the best, and more,   135

    And all the flowers you can both collect,

    And the rest, like parades, and shiny shoes.

PROTEUS

    Why Valentine, what braggartism is this?

VALENTINE

    Oh, what matters when she is all that matters?

    No one matters! Not me, you, or Julia.   140

    She is alone.

PROTEUS

    Then leave her alone.

VALENTINE

    Not for the world! Why child, she is my own,

    And I'm as rich in having such a jewel,

    As twenty seas, if all their sand were pearl,   145

    The water, wine, and the rocks pure gold.

    Forgive me, that I do not dream on you,

Because you see me dote upon my Love.
Her Father prefers Thurio, for his
"huuuuuuuuuuuuuge" wealth, nothing earned,   150
But he's gone with her, so I must after,
For Love, you know, is full of jealousy.

PROTEUS

But she loves you?

VALENTINE

Yes! And we are betrothed! Soon to fly away,
With all the magic of a higher Love,   155
But first things first, I must climb her window,
The ladder made of rope, and clever disguises
Plotted, and agreed on for my happiness.
Good Proteus go with me to my chamber,
Help me, calm me down, tell me what you think!   160

PROTEUS

Go on ahead. I shall find you.
I must back to the road, to unpack
Some of my stuff. I need it. Very important.

VALENTINE

Will you hurry?

PROTEUS

I will.   165

Exit Valentine

PROTEUS

And as one heat expels another heat,
Or as one nail by strength drives out another.
So the remembrance of my former Love
Is by a newer object quite forgotten!
Is this mine, or Valentine's praise?   170
Her true perfection, or my false transgression
That makes me reasonless, to reason thus?

She is fair. And so is Julia that I Love!
That I did Love, for now my Love is thaw'd,
Which like a waxen image against a fire   175
Leaves no impression of the thing it was.
Methinks my zeal to Valentine is cruel!
And that I Love him not as I once did,
O, but I Love his lady too too much,
And that's the reason I Love him so little.   180
How shall I dote on her, knowing his secret,
When I was ignorant first meeting her?
She's a picture of high art, new to me,
And that has dazzled my reason's light.
How can I hope for her, when I look at that!   185
There is no reason but I shall be blind.
If I can check my criminal Love, I will,
If not, to win her hand I'll use my skill.

Exit

ACT 2 ◆ SCENE 5

Enter Speed, Lance, and Crab

SPEED

Lance! Welcome to Milan, my weirdest friend.

CRAB

Hi!

SPEED

Crab!

LANCE

Speed! Lie not to yourself, sweet youth, for I am not welcome. I reckon this always, that a man is never undone till   5
he be hang'd, nor never welcome to a place, till some certain
shot be paid, and the Hostess say welcome.

SPEED

Come on then, I'll take you to the Ale house.

(*remembers*)

But first, Julia.

LANCE (*looks about*)

Where?   10

SPEED

How did the gentle soul leave his great Love?

Shall she marry him?

LANCE

No.

SPEED

How then? Shall he marry her?

LANCE

Nope, neither.   .   15

SPEED

What, are they broken?

LANCE

No.

SPEED

Then what's the problem!

LANCE

What problem? No problem.

SPEED

But Julia! Will there be a wedding?   20

LANCE

Ask my dog, if he says yes, it will. If he says no, it will.

If he wags his tail and say nothing, it will.

SPEED

The conclusion is that it will!

LANCE

It will!

37

Alehouse?   25
SPEED
    We will.

                                Exit

                        ACT 2 ◆ SCENE 6
                            Enter Proteus

PROTEUS
    To leave my Julia, shall I be forsworn?
    To Love fair Sylvia, shall I be forsworn?
    To wrong my Friend, I shall be much forsworn.
    And even that passion which gave me first my oath
    Provokes me to this threefold perjury.   5
    Love wished me swear, and Love wishes me forswear.
    O sweet suggesting Love, if you have sinned,
    Teach me, your tempted subject, to excuse it.
    At first I did adore a twinkling star,
    But now I worship a blinding sun.   10
    Ill-considered vows may be considerably broken,
    And he is a fool, that wants a perfect mind,
    To learn his mind, then exchange the bad for better.
    Fuck my irreverent tongue, to call her bad,
    Whose sovereignty so oft have you preferred,   15
    With twenty thousand soul confirming oaths.
    I cannot leave to Love, and yet I do.
    But there I leave to Love, where I should Love.
    Julia I lose, and Valentine I lose,
    If I keep them, I must lose myself!   20
    If I lose them, then find myself by their loss,
    For Valentine, myself. For Julia, Sylvia.
    I to myself am dearer than a Friend,
    For Love is still most precious in itself,

And Sylvia, light of heaven that made her fair,   25
Shows Julia but a plain country girl.
I will forget that Julia is alive!
Remembering only that my Love to her is dead.
And Valentine I'll call my enemy,
Fighting for Sylvia as a sweeter Friend.   30
I cannot be loyal to myself,
Without some treachery to Valentine.
This night he plans with a rope ladder
To climb perfect Sylvia's chamber window,
Myself will help his enemy, myself.   35
Now presently I'll give her Father notice
Of their disguising and pretended flight.
Who, all enraged, will banish Valentine,
He intends Thurio shall wed his daughter.
But with Valentine gone, I'll quickly devise   40
By some sly trick, stupid Thurio's end.
Love lend me wings! To make my actions swift,
As you have lent me myself, the greatest gift.

Exit

ACT 2 ◆ SCENE 7

Enter Julia and Lucetta

JULIA

Save me from myself, gentle Lucetta!
Teach me, and tell me some good plan
How may I with my Honor undertake
A journey to my loving Proteus?

LUCETTA

Alas, the way to his heart is exhausting.   5

JULIA

A true devoted pilgrim is not tired

To measure Kingdoms with his feeble steps,
Much less shall she that has Love's wings to fly,
And when the flight is made to one so dear,
Of such divine perfection as Sir Proteus. 10

LUCETTA

Better wait, till Proteus makes his return.

JULIA

Don't you see how his looks are my soul's food?
Pity my emptiness!

LUCETTA

Yeah.

JULIA

The more you choke Love, the more it squeals. 15

LUCETTA

Right.

JULIA

But when I'm free to Love, and do it loudly,
He makes sweet music with every footstep,
Gives a gentle kiss to each bird and tree
He steps on in his pilgrimage. 20
And so by many winding nooks he strays
With willing sport to the wild Ocean.
Then let me go, and hinder not my course,
I'll be as patient as a gentle stream,
And make a pastime of each weary step, 25
Till the last step has brought me to my Love,
And there I'll rest, as after much turmoil
A blessed soul does in Heaven!

LUCETTA

But what will you wear?! There's danger in dresses.

JULIA

Not like a woman, for I want to avoid 30

40

The violent sport of lascivious men.
Gentle Lucetta, fit me with such clothes
As may befit some innocent schoolboy.
How fantastic, to become a boy!
More fun than being Julia.   35

LUCETTA

What fashion, madam, shall I make your pants?

JULIA

Why, whatever fashion you like best, Lucetta.

LUCETTA

These days manly leggings are not worth a sock,
Unless you have a codpiece to stick socks in.

JULIA

Out, out, gentle wench! How embarrassing!   40
Lucetta, as you love me let me have
What you think is good, and most mannerly.
But tell me, how will the world repute me
For undertaking so crazy a journey?
I fear me it will make me scandalized.   45

LUCETTA

If you think so, then stay at home, and go not.

JULIA

No, that I will not.

LUCETTA

Then never dream on infamy, but go.
If Proteus likes your journey, when you come,
Care not who is displeased, when you are gone.   50
I fear me it's he who will be displeased.

JULIA

That is the least, Lucetta of my fear!
A thousand oaths, an Ocean of his tears,
promise me to my Proteus.

LUCETTA

These feelings are servants to deceitful men. 55

JULIA

Base men, that use them to so base effect.

But truer stars did govern Proteus's birth,

His words are bonds, his oaths are oracles,

His Love sincere, his thoughts immaculate,

His tears, pure messengers, sent from his heart, 60

His heart, as far from fraud, as heaven from earth!

LUCETTA

Pray heaven he prove so when you come to him.

JULIA

Now, if you love me, do him not that wrong

To question his truth with such attitude.

Only deserve my Love, by loving him, 65

And immediately go with me to my chamber

To take a note of what I stand in need of

To furnish me upon my longing journey.

All that is mine I leave in your hands,

My goods, my lands, my reputation, 70

Only, in lieu thereof, send me on my way.

Come, answer not, but to it presently,

I am impatient the longer we stay.

Exit

ACT 3 ◆ SCENE 1

Enter Duke, Thurio, and Proteus

DUKE

    Sir Thurio, give us leave, I pray awhile,

    We have some secrets to confer about.

                Exit Thurio

    Now tell me Proteus, what's your will with me?

PROTEUS

    My gracious Lord, what I have discovered,

    The law of friendship asks me to conceal,   5

    But when I call to mind your gracious favors

    Done to me, undeserving as I am,

    My duty pricks me on to utter that

    Which no worldly good or torture would rip from me.

    Know worthy Prince, Sir Valentine, my Friend   10

    Intends to steal away your daughter this night!

    Myself against my will made witness.

    I know you have determined to bestow her

    On Thurio, whom your gentle daughter hates,

    Alas! Should she be stolen away from you,   15

    It would be much vexation to your age!

    Thus, for my duty's sake I rather chose

    To drown my Friend in his deceit,

    Than, by concealing it, heap on your head

    A thousand sorrows, which would weigh you down,   20

    Being undefeated, to your timeless grave.

DUKE

    Proteus! I thank you for your honest care,

    Which to reward, command me while I live.

This Love of theirs, myself have often seen,
Sneakily when they judged me fast asleep, 25
And often I have plotted to forbid
Sir Valentine her company, and my Court.
But fearing lest my jealous heart might err,
And so, unworthily disgrace the man,
A rashness I ever yet have hated in others, 30
I gave him gentle looks, thereby to find
That which you have disclosed to me now.
And that you may perceive my fear of this,
Knowing that tender youth is soon suggested,
I nightly lodge her in an upper tower, 35
Whereof, myself has always kept the key.
And thence she cannot be stolen away!

PROTEUS

Know, noble Lord, they have devised a means.
How her window he will clamber up,
And with a rope ladder fetch her down. 40
For which, the youthful lover now is gone,
And this way comes he with it presently.
Where, if it please you, you may intercept him.
But good, my Lord, do it so cunningly
That my discovery be not aimed at, 45
For, Love of you, not hate unto my Friend,
Has made me a snitch of this fakery.

DUKE

Upon mine Honor, he shall never know
That I had any light of this from you.

PROTEUS

Adieu, my Lord, Sir Valentine is coming. 50

Exit Proteus
Enter Valentine

44

DUKE

Sir Valentine, why run away so fast?

VALENTINE

Please it your Grace, there is a Messenger

That stays to post my letters to my friends,

And I am going to deliver them.

DUKE

Be they important?   55

VALENTINE

Ah, just notes about how happy I am.

Being at your Court. With you. And your … s.

DUKE

Oh then no matter, stay with me awhile,

I want to talk to you of some affairs

That touch me deep, can you keep a secret?   60

It's not unknown to you, that I have sought

To match my Friend Sir Thurio, to my daughter.

VALENTINE

I know it well, my Lord, and sure the match

Were rich and honorable. Besides, the gentleman

Is full of Virtue, Bounty, Worth, and Qualities   65

Beseeming such a Wife, as your fair daughter.

A pity she dislikes him so.

DUKE

No, trust me, she is peevish, sullen, forward,

Proud, disobedient, stubborn, lacking duty,

Neither regarding that she is my child,   70

Not fearing me as if I were her Father.

And may I say to you, this pride of hers,

Much remarked upon has poisoned my Love,

And where I thought the remnant of mine age

Should have been cherished by her child-like duty,   75

45

I am fully resolved to take a wife,
And turn her out, to who will take her in.
Then let her beauty be her wedding dowry.
For she does not care for me, or my name.
VALENTINE
What would your Grace have me to do in this? 80
DUKE
There is a Lady in the city here.
Whom I affect but she is nice, and coy,
And naught esteems my aged eloquence.
Now therefore would I have you to my Tutor!
For long ago I forgot how to court, 85
Besides, the fashion of the time is changed.
How, and which way I may bestow myself
To be regarded in her sun-bright eye.
VALENTINE
If words fall flat, win her with sparkly gifts,
Dumb jewels often in their silent kind 90
Are quicker than rhymes, and move a woman's mind.
DUKE
But she did reject the gift I sent her!
VALENTINE
A woman sometimes rejects what she wants most.
Send her another, never give up. Never,
For "no" at first, makes "yes okay" the better, 95
And if she glares, it's not in hate of you,
But rather to get more sweet songs from you.
If she screams, it's not to have you gone,
For why, the fools are mad, if left alone.
Take no repulse, whatever she does say, 100
For "get you gone," she does not mean "away."
Flatter, praise, joke, lie, list her best, ah, graces,

But never so wild, they have angel's faces,
That man who has a tongue, I say is no man
If with his tongue he cannot win a woman.   105

DUKE

But alas, she is promised by her choice,
To a youthful Gentleman of worth,
And keeps herself safe, away from men,
That no man can reach her chamber by day.

VALENTINE

Why then, Sir, I would surprise her by night.   110

DUKE

The doors are bolted shut, and keys kept safe.
No man can win her in the dark of night!

VALENTINE

Why, what about her window?

DUKE

Her chamber is aloft, far from the ground,
And built so smooth, that one cannot climb it   115
Without apparent hazard of his life.

VALENTINE

Then a ladder, bravely made of rope
To throw up, with a pair of metal hooks,
That would offer safe-ish passage into Juliet,
So bold Romeo would adventure it.   120

DUKE

Now as you are a Gentlemanly man,
Advise me, where may I find such a Ladder?

VALENTINE

When would you use it? Pray sir, tell me that.

DUKE

Tonight. For Love is like a child who longs,
For everyone and thing he can grab.   125

VALENTINE

I'll get you such a ladder by … seven.

DUKE

But tell me, tutor, I will go alone,

How does one carry such a long ladder?

VALENTINE

It will be light, my Lord, that you may hide it,

Under a cloak of any length.   130

DUKE

A cloak as long as yours will do the job?

VALENTINE

Yes, my good Lord.

DUKE

Then let me see your cloak,

I'll get me one of such another length.

VALENTINE

Why any cloak will do the job, my Lord.   135

DUKE

Will it suit me, to wear a cloak like that?

Please let me try yours, just let me feel it.

(*pulling off the cloak, Duke reveals a rope ladder and a paper*)

What letter is this same? What's here? "To Sylvia"?

Well, well, so much I've learnt today, and more.

If I'm so bold as to open this bravery.   140

(*reads*)

"*My thoughts do rest with my Sylvia nightly,*

They are painted clowns, that I send them flying.

Oh, could their master come, and go as lightly,

Himself would sleep where senseless they are lying.

My godly thoughts, in your pure bosom rest them,   145

While I, their King, that demands their silence

Does curse the laughter, that grace has blessed them,

48

I myself, jealous, of my clowns' fun fortune.
I hate myself, for they are sent by me,
That they should play where me, their Lord should be."   150
What's here?
"Sylvia, this night I will liberate thee."
Seems earnest, and here's a ladder for the deed.
Why foolish jester, you are the King of Clowns,
In your dreams do you drive the bright clown cart?   155
And with your daring folly trick the world?
Will you reach stars, because they shine on you?
Go vile intruder, over indulgent joke,
Perform your fake smile on smaller friends,
And think my patience, more than you deserve,   160
Is privilege for your departure hence.
Thank me for this, more than for all the favors
Which, all too much, I have bestowed on thee!
But if you linger in my territories
By heaven, my wrath shall far exceed the Love   165
I ever gave my daughter, or yourself.
Jump! Fly! I will not hear your stupid song,
But as you Love your life, run fast! Begone!
                              Exit Duke

VALENTINE

And why not death, it's better than living torment?
To die, is to be banished from myself,   170
And Sylvia is myself. Banished from her
Is self from self. A deadly banishment!
What light, is light, if Sylvia be not seen?
What joy is joy, if Sylvia be not by?
Unless it be to think that she is by   175
And feed upon the shadow of perfection.
Except I be by Sylvia in the night,

There is no music in the Nightingale.
Unless I look on Sylvia in the day,
There is no day for me to look upon. 180
She is my essence, and I leave to be,
If I be not by her fair influence
Fostered, illumined, cherished, kept alive.
I fly not death, to fly his deadly doom,
Hide here and I will meet violent strife, 185
But if I fly, I fly away from life!

Enter Proteus and Lance

PROTEUS

Run, gentle child, run, and seek him out!

LANCE

Holy shit! Holy shit!

PROTEUS

What seest thou?

LANCE

Him we go to find, 190
There's not a hair on's head, but 'tis a Valentine!

PROTEUS

Valentine?

VALENTINE

No.

PROTEUS

Who then? His Spirit?

VALENTINE

Neither, 195

PROTEUS

What then?

VALENTINE

Nothing.

LANCE

Can nothing speak? Master, shall I punch?

PROTEUS

Who would you punch?

LANCE

Nothing.   200

PROTEUS

Villain, stop it.

LANCE

Why Sir, I'll punch nothing, I pray you.

PROTEUS

Servant, I say resist! Friend Valentine, a word.

VALENTINE

My ears are clogged and cannot hear good news,

So much of bad already has stuffed them.   205

PROTEUS

Then in dumb silence will I bury mine,

For they are harsh, dissonant, and bad.

VALENTINE

Is Sylvia dead?

PROTEUS

No, Valentine.

VALENTINE

No Valentine indeed for sacred Sylvia,   210

Has she abandoned me?

PROTEUS

No, Valentine.

VALENTINE

No Valentine, if Sylvia have abandoned me.

What is your news?

LANCE

Sir, there is a proclamation, you are vanished.   215

PROTEUS

That you are banished.
Oh that's the news,
From hence, from Sylvia, and from me your Friend.

VALENTINE

Oh, I have fed upon this woe already,
And now excess of it will make me vomit. 220
Does Sylvia know that I am banished?

PROTEUS

Yes. Yes, and she has offered to the doom,
Which established stands in effectual force,
A sea of melting pearl, which some call tears,
Those at her Father's churlish feet she tendered, 225
With them upon her knees, her humble self,
Wringing her hands, whose softness so became them,
As if just now they waxed pale for woe.
But neither bended knees, pure hands held up,
Sad sighs, deep groans, nor silver shedding tears 230
Could impale her heartless Sir.
But Valentine, if he be found, must die.
Besides, when she begged for you like a baby,
He stuffed her in a high chair, lone and squealing
Shouting bitter threats of growing old there. 235

VALENTINE

She is grounded?

PROTEUS

She is.

VALENTINE

No more! Unless the next word that you speak
Has some medicinal power upon my life,
If so, I pray you sing it in my ear, 240
A final song to my endless sadness.

PROTEUS

    Well, you cannot help what you cannot help,

    Look only to what you can, and friends like me.

    Time and space is the doctor of all good.

    If you stay, you cannot see your Love.   245

    Besides, your staying will get you killed.

    Hope is a lover's light, walk on with that

    And hold it close, against tragic thoughts.

    Write poems in the wild, and send them here

    Send them to me and they will be delivered   250

    Straight to the heart of your great Love.

    The time for complaint is long gone.

    Come, I'll help you to the city gate.

    And there we'll part, with a plan of action,

    To slay all that concerns your Love affairs.   255

    As you Love Sylvia, then think of her,

    Believe your danger and along with me.

VALENTINE

    Dear, gentle Lance, if you see unspeedy Speed,

    Please tell him to meet me at the north gate.

PROTEUS

    Go drunkard, find him out. Come, Valentine.   260

VALENTINE

    Oh my dear Sylvia! Hapless Valentine!

               Exit Valentine and Proteus

LANCE

    I am a fool, yes, but my master is a fake. He keeps secrets

    from his friends but so do I! I am in Love too! And wild

    horses shall not take that from me, or who it is I Love. And

    yet it is a woman. But what woman, I will not tell anyone. 265

    And yet it is a milk maid. Yet it is not a "maid," for she has a

    reputation. Yet it is a maid, for she is her master's maid, and squeezes tits for wages. She has more qualities than her cows, which is much in a basic human.

Pulls out paper

Here is the catalog of her condition. "Item. She can fetch 270 and carry." Why a horse can do the same, no, a horse cannot fetch, but only carry! Therefore, she is better than a horse. "Item. She can milk," look you, a sweet virtue in a maid with clean hands.

Enter Speed

SPEED

How now Mr. Lance! You have made it out of the alehouse. 275 What news?

LANCE

News of the alehouse? It has ale.

SPEED

What news then in your paper?

LANCE

The most tragic news that ever you heard.

SPEED

Let me look! 280

LANCE

You cannot read. Now that is most tragic.

SPEED

You lie! I can.

Speed takes the paper and reads

SPEED

"Item. She can milk."

LANCE

Yes, yes, she can.

SPEED

"Item, she can sew." 285

LANCE

That's as much as to say, "Can she so?"

SPEED

"Item. She can knit."

LANCE

What need a man care for a sock with a wench,

When she can knit him a sock?

SPEED

"Item, she can wash and scrub." 290

LANCE

A special virtue. For then she need not be washed, and scrubbed.

SPEED

"Item. She can spin."

LANCE

Then may I set the world on wheels, when she can spin for

her living!

SPEED

"Item, she hath many nameless virtues." 295

LANCE

That's as much as to say bastard virtues. That knowing not

their fathers, have no names.

SPEED

"Here follow her vices."

LANCE

Wait! You *can* read.

SPEED

"Item, she is not to be fasting in respect of her breath." 300

LANCE

Well, that fault may be mended with a breakfast, read on.

SPEED

"Item, she hath a sweet mouth."

LANCE

That makes amends for her sour breath.

SPEED

"Item, she talks in her sleep."

LANCE

It's no matter for that, so she sleep not when she talks.   305

SPEED

"Item, she is slow in words."

LANCE

Oh villain, that set this down among her vices!

To be slow in words, is a woman's only virtue.

I pray you out with it, and place it for her chief virtue.

SPEED

"Item, she is proud."   310

LANCE

Out with that too. It was Eve's legacy, and cannot be taken from her.

SPEED

"Item, she has no teeth."

LANCE

I care not for that either! Because I Love crusts.

SPEED

"Item, she is nasty."   315

LANCE

That's fine, she has no teeth to bite.

SPEED

"Item, she will often praise her liquor."

LANCE

If her liquor be good, she shall. If she will not, I will, for good things should be praised.

SPEED

"Item, she has more hair than wit, and more faults than hairs,   320 and more toes than faults."

LANCE

Stop there. I'll have her. She is mine.

In these days of great Loves, nothing is impossible.

SPEED

Great Loves?

LANCE

Oh yes, your master waits for you at the north gate.   325

SPEED

For me?

LANCE

He is banished.

SPEED

Banished! And I must go to him? Shit.

LANCE

Yes you must run, unspeedy Speed, as he calls you.

SPEED

Does he? What a ...   330

LANCE

Go!

Speed exits, tripping
Lance laughs

INTERMISSION

ACT 3 ◆ SCENE 2

Enter Duke and Thurio

DUKE

Sir Thurio, fear not, she will Love you, only you,

Now Valentine is banish'd from her sight.

THURIO

Since his exile she despises me more,

Rejects my company and screams at me,
That I am desperate to obtain her.   5
DUKE
A little time will melt her frozen thoughts,
And worthless Valentine shall be forgot.

Enter Proteus

How now Sir Proteus, is your countryman,
Gone, according to our Proclamation?
PROTEUS
Gone, my good Lord.   10
DUKE
My daughter takes his going grievously?
PROTEUS
A little time, my Lord, will kill that grief.
DUKE
So I believe but Thurio thinks not so.
Proteus, you have shown much bright potential,
A great mind, and a great friend to talk to.   15
You remind me of myself at your age.
PROTEUS
Let me live up to that, and prove loyal,
Tell all and I will keep it to myself.
DUKE
You know how much I hope for a tight knot,
Between Sir Thurio, and my daughter?   20
PROTEUS
I do, my Lord.
DUKE
And also, I think, you are not ignorant,
How she opposes him against my will?
PROTEUS
She did my Lord, when Valentine was here.

DUKE

 Yes, and perversely, she perseveres so.   25

 What might we do to make the girl forget

 The Love of Valentine, and Love Sir Thurio?

PROTEUS

 The best way is, to slander Valentine,

 With falsehood, cowardice, and poor descent.

 Three things that women highly hold in hate.   30

DUKE

 Yes, but she'll think, that it is spoke in hate.

PROTEUS

 Sure, if his enemy deliver it.

 Therefore it must with circumstance be spoken

 By one who she knows only as his Friend.

DUKE

 Then you must undertake to slander him.   35

PROTEUS

 And that, my Lord, I shall be loath to do.

 'Tis an ill office for a Gentleman,

 Especially against his very Friend.

DUKE

 Where your good word cannot advantage him,

 Your slander never can damage him.   40

PROTEUS

 You have prevailed, my Lord. If I can do it

 By ought that I can speak in his dispraise,

 She shall not long continue Love to him.

 But say this plucks her Love from Valentine,

 It follows not that she will Love Sir Thurio.   45

THURIO

 Therefore, as you unwind her Love from him,

 Least it should entangle, and be good to none,

You must provide to lavish it on me,
Which must be done, by praising me as much
As you, with such skill, slander sir Valentine.   50
DUKE
And Proteus, we dare trust you in this kind,
Because we know, on Valentine's report,
You are already Love's addict,
And cannot soon revolt and change your mind.
Upon this warrant shall you have access,   55
Where you with Sylvia, may confer at large —
For she is lumpish, heavy, melancholy,
And for your Friend's sake, will be glad of you —
Where you may temper her, by your persuasion,
To hate young Valentine, and Love my Friend.   60
PROTEUS
As much as I can do, I will perform.
But you, Sir Thurio, are no match for me.
You must pluck strings, to tangle her desires
Write wailful Sonnets, whose clerkly rhymes
Ought be full fraught with rhyming vowels.   65
DUKE
Yes, much is the force of heavenly poetry.
PROTEUS
Say that upon the altar of her beauty
You sacrifice your tears, your sighs, your heart.
Write till your ink be dry. And with your tears
Wet it again, and frame some feeling line,   70
That may discover such integrity.
For Orpheus's Lute was strung with Poet's guts,
Whose golden touch could soften blades and stones.
Visit by night your lady's chamber window
With many loud instruments, to surprise her.   75

Wake the night's dead silence with lively music!

Yes! She will appreciate the gesture.

This, or else nothing, will win her.

DUKE

This self-restraint shows you have been in Love.

THURIO (*to Proteus*)

And I'll give your advice a shot tonight!   80

Let us find some blow hards, well skilled in Music.

I have a Sonnet, that will do the job,

Being worthy of your … talents.

DUKE

About it, Gentlemen.

PROTEUS

We'll wait upon your Grace 'til dinner, and dessert,   85

And afterward think about makin' moves.

DUKE

I will excuse you. Go.

Exit

ACT 4 ◆ SCENE 1

Enter certain Outlaws

O' ONE

Fellows, stand fast. I see a voice.

O' TWO

If there be ten, hide not, but down with 'em.

Enter Valentine and Speed

O' THREE

Stand sir, and throw us that you have about ye.

If not, we'll make you sit, and rifle you!

SPEED (*to Valentine*)

Sir we are fucked! These are the villains   5

That gentle travelers do fear so much!

VALENTINE

My friends.

O' ONE

That's not so, sir! We are your enemies.

O' TWO

Peace. We'll hear him.

VALENTINE

Then know that I have little wealth to lose.   10

I am a man, stripped naked by my foes,

My riches are these unfashionable clothes,

Which, if you should take them, (*pointing to Speed*) or even him,

You take the sum and substance that I have.

O' TWO

Where travel you?   15

VALENTINE

To Verona.

63

O' ONE

Whence came you?

VALENTINE

From Milan.

O' THREE

Been there long?

VALENTINE

Some six months. And longer might I have stayed,   20

If crooked fortune had not ruined everything.

O' ONE

Were you banished?

VALENTINE

I was.

O' TWO

For what offense?

VALENTINE

For that which now torments me to rehearse.   25

I killed a man, whose death I much repent,

But yet I stabbed him manfully, in fight,

Without false advantage, or treachery.

O' ONE

Why never regret it! If it were done so.

But were you banished for such a misdemeanor?   30

VALENTINE

I was, and I am glad of such a fate.

O' TWO

Have you been touched, by the divine?

VALENTINE

My childish travels have made me happy,

Or else I might have worked, and hated it.

O' ONE

He can be our King! Sirs, a word.   35

ACT 4 ◆ SCENE 1

The Outlaws step aside to talk

SPEED

Gentle friend, be one of them.

It's an honorable kind of thievery.

VALENTINE

Chill Speedy!

O' THREE

Tell no one, but some of us are Gentlemen,

Such is the fury of ungoverned youth   40

Thrust from the company of awful men.

Myself was banished from fair Verona,

For attempted kidnapping of a Lady,

A distant relative, allied to the Duke.

O' TWO

And I from Mantua, for a Gentleman,   45

Who, in my mood, I stabbed unto the heart.

O' ONE

And I, for such like petty crimes as these.

But to the purpose, for we tell our faults,

That they may justify our lawless lives.

And partly seeing you are well bred,   50

With goodly shape. And by your own report,

Gentle-ish, and a man of such perfection,

As we do in our quality much want.

O' TWO

Indeed because you are a banish'd man,

Therefore, above the rest, we answer to you.   55

Are you content to be our General?

To make a virtue of necessity,

And live as we do in this wilderness?

O' THREE

What say thou? Wilt thou join our revolution?

Say yes, and be the captain of us all.   60

We'll do thee homage, and be ruled by thee,

Love thee, as our Commander, and our King.

O' ONE

But if thou decline our gift, we will kill you.

O' TWO

Thou shalt not live, to brag what we have offered.

VALENTINE

I take your offer, and will live with you,   65

Provided that you do no outrages

On silly women, or poor passengers.

O' THREE

No, we detest such vile base practices.

Come, go with us, we'll bring thee to our hideout

And show thee all the treasure we have got.

Which, with ourselves, all rest at thy dispose.

Exit

ACT 4 ◆ SCENE 2

Enter Proteus

PROTEUS

Already I've been false to Valentine,

And now I must be as unjust to Thurio.

Under the deceit of flattering him,

I have days alone with my enchanting Love.

But Sylvia is too fair, too true, too holy,   5

To be corrupted with my worthless gifts.

When I protest true loyalty to her,

She jabs me with my falsehood to my Friend.

When to her beauty I commend my vows,

She reminds me I am betrothed to another,   10

In breaking faith with Julia, whom I loved.

And notwithstanding all her sudden quips,
The least whereof would quell a lover's hope,
Yet red rose like, the more she fights my Love,
The more it flowers, and drops petals on her still.   15

Enter Thurio and Musicians

But here comes Thurio. Now must we to her window,
And give some evening music to her ear.

THURIO

How now, Sir Proteus, are you crept before us?

PROTEUS

Yes gentle Thurio, for you know that Love
Will creep in service, where it cannot go.   20

THURIO

Aye, but I hope, Sir, that you Love not here.

PROTEUS

Sir, but I do. Or else I would be hence.

THURIO

Who, Sylvia?

PROTEUS

True Sylvia, for your sake.

THURIO

I thank you for your own. Now Gentlemen.   25
Let's tune. And to it lustily awhile.

Enter Hotelier and Julia disguised as Sebastian

HOTELIER

Why so sad! Come, we'll have you dancing. I'll bring you to
the music and see the Gentleman that you asked for.

JULIA

But shall I hear him speak?

HOTELIER

You shall.   30

JULIA

That will be music.

Loud music plays, very enthusiastically

HOTELIER

Holy, holy angels.

JULIA

Is he among these?

HOTELIER

Yes, but peace, let's hear them.

The Musicians play and sing

PROTEUS (*singing*)

Who is Sylvia? What is she?   35
That all the boys acclaim her?
Holy, fair, and wise is she,
The heaven such grace did lend her,
That she might admired be.
Is she kind as she is fair?   40
For beauty lives with kindness.
Love doth to her eyes repair,
To help him of his blindness.
And being helped, inhabits there.
Then to Sylvia! Let us sing!   45
That Sylvia is excelling.
She excels each mortal thing
Upon the dull earth dwelling.
To her let us Garlands bring.

HOTELIER

Oh dear! Are you sadder than you were before?   50
How do you, youth? The music likes you not.

JULIA (*as Sebastian*)

You mistake. The musician likes me not.

HOTELIER

Why, my pretty youth?

JULIA (*as Sebastian*)

He plays false, Father.

HOTELIER

How, out of tune on the strings? 55

JULIA (*as Sebastian*)

Not so, but yet

So false that he grieves my very heartstrings.

HOTELIER

You have a quick ear.

JULIA (*as Sebastian*)

Aye, I would I were deaf! It makes me have a slow heart.

HOTELIER

I perceive you delight not in music. 60

JULIA (*as Sebastian*)

Not at all! When it jars so.

HOTELIER

Wow! What fine change is in the music.

JULIA (*as Sebastian*)

Yes, that change is the problem.

HOTELIER

You would have them always play but one thing.

JULIA (*as Sebastian*)

I would always have one play just one thing. 65

But Friend, does this Sir Protcus, that we talk on,

Often entertain this Gentlewoman?

HOTELIER

I tell you what Lance, his help told me,

He loves her out of all reason.

JULIA (*as Sebastian*)

Where is Lance? 70

HOTELIER

Gone to seek his dog, which tomorrow, by his master's great
scheme, he must gift to his lady.

Music ends

JULIA (*as Sebastian*)

Peace, stand aside, the company parts.

Hotelier and Julia step aside

PROTEUS

Sir Thurio, our work is done! And won!

My cunning plan demands your sweetest smile!   75

THURIO (*smiling*)

Where meet we?

PROTEUS

At Saint Gregory's well.

THURIO

Farewell.

Exit Thurio and Musicians

Enter Sylvia, above

PROTEUS

Madam. Good evening to your Ladyship.

SYLVIA

I thank you for your music, gentlemen.   80

Whose voice did I hear above?

PROTEUS

One, Lady, if you knew his pure heart's truth,

You would quickly learn to know him by his voice.

SYLVIA

Sir Proteus, as I take it.

PROTEUS

Sir Proteus, gentle Lady, and your servant.   85

SYLVIA

What's your will?

PROTEUS

    That I may understand yours.

SYLVIA

    You have your wish. My will is even this,

    That presently you go home to your bed.

    You flimsy, misleading, fake, disloyal man.   90

    You think I am so shallow, so naïve,

    To be seduced by your flattery,

    That has deceived so many with your vows?

    Return, return, and make amends with thy Love.

    For me, by this pale queen of night I swear   95

    I am so far from granting your request

    That I despise you, for your wrongful suit,

    And by and by intend to scold myself,

    Even for this time I spend in talking to you!

PROTEUS

    I grant, sweet Love, that I did Love a Lady,   100

    But she is dead.

JULIA

    'Twere false, if I should speak it,

    For I am sure she is not buried.

SYLVIA

    Say that she be, yet your friend, Valentine

    Survives, to whom yourself are witness   105

    I am betroth'd. Are you not ashamed

    To wrong him, with your opportunism?

PROTEUS

    I likewise hear that Valentine is dead.

SYLVIA

    And so suppose am I, for in his grave

    Assure yourself, my Love is buried.   110

PROTEUS

Sweet Lady, let me dig it from the earth.

SYLVIA

Go to your lady's grave and find your place,

Or at the least, bury yourself in hers.

JULIA

He didn't hear that.

PROTEUS

Madam, if your heart be so dogged,   115

Concede me yet your picture for my Love,

The picture that is hanging in your chamber.

To that I'll speak, to that I'll sigh and weep.

For since the substance of your perfect self,

Is else devoted, I am but a shadow,   120

And to your shadow, will I make true Love.

JULIA

If 'twere a substance you would sure deceive it,

And make it but a shadow, as I am.

SYLVIA

I am very loath to be your idol sir.

But, since your dishonesty shall become you well   125

To worship shadows and adore false shapes,

Send to me in the morning, and I'll send it,

And so, goodnight

Exit Sylvia

PROTEUS

I'll sleep as the damned sleep at night,

Who wait for execution at breakfast.   130

Exit Proteus

JULIA (*as Sebastian*)

Friend, will you go?

HOTELIER

I was fast asleep. Is it day?

JULIA (*as Sebastian*)

Not so, but it has been the longest night

And the heaviest I have ever watched.

Exit

ACT 4 ◆ **SCENE 3**

Enter Eglamore

EGLAMORE

This is the house that Madam Sylvia

Entreated me to call and know her mind.

There's some great matter she'd employ me in.

Madam, Madam!

Enter Sylvia, above

SYLVIA

Who calls?   5

EGLAMORE

Your servant, and your Friend.

One that attends your Ladyship's command.

SYLVIA

Sir Eglamore, a thousand times good morrow!

EGLAMORE

As many, worthy lady, to yourself.

According to your ladyship's request,   10

I have come early to know what service

It is your pleasure to command me in.

SYLVIA

Oh Eglamore, you are a Gentleman.

Think not I flatter, for I swear I do not.

Valiant, wise, remorse-full, well accomplish'd.   15

You are not ignorant what dear good will

I bear unto the banish'd Valentine,
Nor how my Father would enforce me marry
Vain Thurio, whom my very soul abhors.
Yourself hast loved, and I have heard thee say   20
No grief did ever come so near thy heart,
As when thy Lady, and thy true Love died,
Upon whose grave thou vow'dst pure chastity.
Sir Eglamore, I would to Mantua,
To Valentine, where I hear he makes camp.   25
And as the ways are dangerous to pass,
I do desire thy worthy company,
Upon whose faith and Honor, I repose.
Urge not my Father's anger, Eglamore.
But think upon my grief, a lady's grief.   30
And on the justice of my flying hence,
To keep me from a most unholy match,
Which heaven and fortune still rewards with plagues.
I do desire thee, even from a heart
As full of sorrows as the Sea of sands,   35
To bear me company and go with me,
If not, to hide what I have said to thee,
That I may venture to depart alone

EGLAMORE

Madam, I pity much your grievances,
Which, since I know they virtuously are placed,   40
I give consent to go along with you,
Risking all I have, in wealth, luck, and hope,
As much I wish all good fortune on you.
When will you go?

SYLVIA

Tonight.   45

EGLAMORE

Where shall I meet you?

SYLVIA

At Friar Patrick's cell,

Where I intend holy Confession.

EGLAMORE

I will not fail your Ladyship.

Good morrow, gentle Lady.   50

SYLVIA

Good morrow, kind Sir Eglamore.

Exit

ACT 4 ◆ SCENE 4

Enter Lance and Crab

LANCE

When a man's servant shall play the mutt with him, look you,
it goes hard. One that I found as a puppy, one that I saved
from drowning, when three or four of his blind brothers and
sisters sunk. I have taught him, even as one would say precisely, "Thus I would teach a dog." And I was sent to deliver   5
him, as a gift from my master to Mistress Sylvia! I came no
sooner into the dining chamber, but he jumps into her dinner, and steals her chicken leg! O, 'Tis a foul thing, when a
dog cannot keep himself in all companies, I would have, as
one should say, one that takes upon him to be a dog indeed,   10
to be, as it were, a dog at all things. If I had not had more wit
than he, to take the blame upon me for what he did, I think
absolutely he'd be hanged for't, sure as I live, he had suffer'd
for't: you shall judge, He thrusts me himself into the company of three or four gentleman like dogs, under the Duke's   15
table, he had not been there a short while, but all the chamber smelled him. "Out with the dog!" said one, "What mutt is

that?" said another. "Throw him out!" said the third, "Hang him up!" said the Duke! I having been acquainted with the smell before, knew it was Crab, and goes me to the fellow that 20
beats the dogs, "Friend," said I, "You mean to beat the dog?" "Hell yes I do!" said he, "You do him the more wrong." Said I, "'Twas I who farted!" And so I did again, to prove it. He speaks to me no more, but throws me out of the chamber. How many masters would do this for his servant? Nope, I tell 25
you I have risked my life to eat puddings he has stolen, otherwise he had been executed. I have replaced with puppets the geese he hath killed, otherwise he had suffered for't. (*to Crab*) Do you even care?!

CRAB

Hi. 30

Enter Proteus and Julia disguised as Sebastian

PROTEUS

Sebastian is your name, I like you well,

And will employ you in some service presently.

JULIA (*as Sebastian*)

In what you please, I'll do what I can.

PROTEUS

I hope you will.

Enter Lance

How now you? Off on a bender? 35

Where have you been these two days loitering?

LANCE

Thing is, Sir, I carried the dog you asked to Mistress Sylvia.

PROTEUS

And what said she to my little jewel?

LANCE

Ah, yes she says your dog was a mongrel, and tells you scruffy thanks is good enough for such a present. 40

PROTEUS

But she received my dog?

LANCE

No indeed she did not.

Here, I have brought him back again.

CRAB

Hi.

PROTEUS

What, didst you offer her this from me?   45

LANCE

Yes Sir, the little puppy was stolen from me

By the hangman's boys in the marketplace,

And then I offer'd her my own, who is a dog

As big as ten of yours and therefore the greater gift.

PROTEUS

Get out of here and find my dog again,   50

Or never return again into my sight.

Away! Do you stay to annoy me more?

Exit Lance with Crab

An employee that still turns me to shame,

Sebastian, I have employed you,

Partly as I have need of such a youth,   55

Who can with some discretion do my business,

For 'Tis no trusting that foolish lout.

But chiefly, for your face, and your behavior,

Which, if my senses deceive me not,

Enjoyed a good childhood, fortune, and truth.   60

Here, I'll explain your most important job,

Go quickly, and take this ring with you,

Deliver it to Madam Sylvia.

She loved me well, who gave this to me.

JULIA (*as Sebastian*)

  It seems you loved her not, to give her no token,   65

  She is dead perhaps?

PROTEUS

  Not so, I think she lives.

JULIA (*as Sebastian*)

  Fuck.

PROTEUS

  Why do you cry fuck?

JULIA (*as Sebastian*)

  I cannot choose but pity her.   70

PROTEUS

  Why do you pity her?

JULIA (*as Sebastian*)

  Because, I think that she loved you as well

  As you do love your Lady Sylvia.

  She dreams on him, that has forgot her love,

  You dote on her, that cares not for your love.   75

  'Tis pity love should be so contrary,

  And thinking on it, makes me cry "Fuck!"

PROTEUS

  Well, give her that ring, and that's that.

  This letter,

  See here's her chamber. Tell my Lady,   80

  I claim the promise of her perfect Picture,

  Your message done, run home to my chamber,

  Where you will find me sad and solitary.

Exit Proteus

JULIA

  How many women would do such a message?

  Fff … Alas poor Proteus, you have entertained   85

  A fox to be the shepherd of your lambs.

Alas, poor fool, why do I pity him
That with his very heart despises me?
Because he loves her, he despises me,
Because I Love him, I must pity him.   90
This ring I gave him, when he parted from me,
To bind him to remember my good will,
And now am I, unhappy Messenger,
To plead for that, which I would not obtain.
To carry that, which I would have refused,   95
To praise his faith, which I would have dispraised.
I am my Master's true confirmed Love,
But cannot be true servant to my Master,
Unless I prove false traitor to myself.
Yet will I woo for him, but yet so coldly,   100
As heaven it knows, I would not have him win.

Enter Sylvia

JULIA (*as Sebastian*)

Gentlewoman, good day. I pray you be my mean
To bring me where to speak with Madam Sylvia.

SYLVIA

What would you with her, if that I be she?

JULIA (*as Sebastian*)

If you be she, I do entreat your patience   105
To hear me speak the message I am sent on.

SYLVIA

From whom?

JULIA (*as Sebastian*)

From my Master, Sir Proteus, Madam.

SYLVIA

Oh, he sends you for a Picture?

JULIA (*as Sebastian*)

Yes, Madam.   110

SYLVIA

Ursula, bring my Picture there,

Go, give your Master this. Tell him from me,

One Julia, that his changing thoughts forget,

Would better fit his bed, than this false idol.

JULIA (*as Sebastian*)

Madam, please you read this Letter, 115

Julia gives Sylvia a paper

Pardon me, madam, I have

Deliver'd you a paper that I should not,

This is the Letter to your Ladyship.

Julia takes back the first paper and hands Sylvia another.

SYLVIA

I ask you let me look on that again.

JULIA (*as Sebastian*)

It may not be, good Madam, pardon me. 120

SYLVIA

There, hold.

I will not look upon your Master's lines,

I know they are dripping with declarations,

And full of newfound oaths, which he will break

As easily, as I do tear his paper. 125

Julia hands her the ring

JULIA (*as Sebastian*)

Madam, he sends your Ladyship this ring.

SYLVIA

The more shame for him, that he sends it me,

For I have heard him say a thousand times,

His Julia gave it him at his departure!

Though his false finger have tarnished the ring, 130

Mine I shall not do his Julia so much wrong.

JULIA

She thanks you.

SYLVIA

What did you say?

JULIA (*as Sebastian*)

I thank you, Madam, that you think on her.

Poor Gentlewoman, my Master wrongs her much.   135

SYLVIA

Do you know her?

JULIA (*as Sebastian*)

Almost as well as I do know myself.

To think upon her woes I do protest

That I have wept a hundred million times.

SYLVIA

She thinks her sweet Proteus has forsaken her?   140

JULIA (*as Sebastian*)

I think she does, and that's her cause of sorrow.

SYLVIA

What is she like?

JULIA (*as Sebastian*)

About my height, for in a play at Verona's Got Talent,

My youth got me to play the woman's part,

And I was trimm'd in Madam Julia's gown,   145

Which served me as fit, by all men's judgements,

As if the garment had been made for me.

Therefore I know she is about my height,

And at that time I made her weep a good,

For I did play a lamentable part.   150

Madam, 'twas Juliet, passioning

For Romeo's perjury, and unjust flight,

Which I so lively acted with my tear,

That my poor mistress moved by my performance,

Wept bitterly, and would I might be dead, 155
If in thought I felt not her very sorrow.

SYLVIA

She is beholding to you, gentle youth.
Alas, poor Lady, desolate and left!
I weep myself to think upon your words,
Here youth. There is my purse, I give thee this 160
For thy sweet mistress's sake, because you love her.
Farewell.

JULIA (*as Sebastian*)

And she shall thank you for it, if ever you know her.

Exit Sylvia

A virtuous gentlewoman, mild, and beautiful.
Here is her Picture, let me see, I think 165
If I had such a necklace, this face of mine
Were full as lovely, as is this of hers,
And yet the Painter flatter'd her a little,
Unless I flatter with myself too much.
Her eyes are gray as glass, and so are mine. 170
What should it be that he loves in her,
That I can make better in myself?
If this fond Love were not a blinded god.
Come shadow, come, and take this shadow up,
Is it your rival, 175
O you senseless form,
You will be worshiped, kissed, loved, and adored.
I'll use you kindly, for your Mistress's sake
That used me so, or else by Love, I vow,
I should have scratched out your unseeing eyes, 180
To make my Master out of Love with you.

Exit

ACT 5 ◆ SCENE 1

Enter Eglamore

EGLAMORE

The Sun begins to guild the western sky,

And now it is about the very hour

That Sylvia, at Friar Patrick's cell should meet me,

She will not fail, for lovers come on time,

Unless it be to come early,   5

So passionately they wait their expedition.

Enter Sylvia

See where she comes. Lady, a happy evening!

SYLVIA

Amen, Amen. Go on, good Eglamore.

Outside the safety of the Abbey wall,

I fear I am being followed by spies.   10

EGLAMORE

Fear not, the forest is not three miles off,

If we make it there, we are safe enough.

Exit

ACT 5 ◆ SCENE 2

Enter Thurio, Proteus, and Julia disguised as Sebastian

THURIO

Sir Proteus, what says Sylvia to my suit?

PROTEUS

Oh Sir, I find her milder than she was,

And yet she takes exceptions at your person.

THURIO

What? That my leg is too long?

PROTEUS

    No, that it is too little.   5

THURIO

    I'll wear a boot, to make it somewhat rounder.

JULIA (*aside*)

    But Love loves what it loves, hates what it hates.

THURIO

    What says she of my face?

PROTEUS

    She says it is a fair one.

THURIO

    Then she lies, or you do. My face is strange.   10

PROTEUS

    But pearls are fair, and the old saying is,

    Strangest are pearls, in beauteous Ladies' eyes.

JULIA (*aside*)

    'Tis true, such pearls as put out lady's eyes,

    For I had rather wink, then look on them.

THURIO

    How likes she my discourse?   15

PROTEUS

    Ill. When you talk of war.

THURIO

    But well, when I discourse of Love and peace?

JULIA (*aside*)

    But better indeed, when you hold your peace.

THURIO

    What says she to my valor?

PROTEUS

    Oh sir, she makes no doubt of that.   20

JULIA (*aside*)

    She needs not, when she knows it cowardice.

THURIO

What says she to my birth?

PROTEUS

That you are well derived.

JULIA (*aside*)

True, from a Gentleman, to a fool.

THURIO

Considers she my Possessions?   25

PROTEUS

Oh, yes, and pities them.

THURIO

Why?

JULIA (*aside*)

That such an idiot should owe them.

PROTEUS

That they are all invested.

JULIA (*as Sebastian*)

Here comes the Duke.   30

Enter Duke

DUKE

How now sir Proteus, how now Thurio?

Which of you saw Eglamore of late?

THURIO

Not I.

PROTEUS

Nor I.

DUKE

Saw you my daughter?   35

PROTEUS

Neither.

DUKE

Why then,

She's fled unto that peasant, Valentine,
And Eglamore is in her Company.
Dispatch, sweet Gentlemen, and follow me.   40

Exit Duke

THURIO

Why, this it is to be a peevish girl
Who flees her fortune when it follows her,
I'll after, more to be revenged on Eglamore
Then for the Love of reckless Sylvia.

Exit Thurio

PROTEUS

And I will follow, more for Sylvia's Love   45
Than hate of Eglamore that goes with her.

Exit Proteus

JULIA

And I will follow, more to cross that Love
Than hate for Sylvia, that is gone for Love.

Exit

ACT 5 ◆ SCENE 3

Enter Sylvia and Outlaws

O' ONE

Come, come, be patient,

We must bring you to our Captain.

SYLVIA

A thousand more shit storms than this one

Have taught me how to deal patiently with this.

O' TWO

Come, bring her away.   5

O' ONE

Where is the Gentleman that was with her?

O' THREE

Being nimble footed, he has outrun us.
But Moyses and Valerius follow him.
Go thou with her to the West end of the wood,
There is our Captain. We'll follow him that's fled,   10
The Thicket is beset, he cannot escape.

Exit O' Two and O' Three

O' ONE

Come, I must bring you to our Captain's cave.
Fear not, he bears an honorable mind,
And will not use a woman lawlessly.

SYLVIA

O Valentine, I endure this for you.   15

Exit

ACT 5 ♦ SCENE 4

Enter Valentine

VALENTINE

How use does breed a habit in a man?
This shadowy desert, unfrequented woods
I better enjoy than a busy, bustling city.
Here can I sit alone, unseen by any,
And to the Nightingale's saddest songs,   5
Tune my distresses, and record my woes.
O thou that dost inhabit in my breast,
Leave not the mansion so long vacant,
Lest growing ruinous, the building fall,
And leave no memory of what it was,   10
Repair me with thy presence, Sylvia.
Thou gentle nymph, cherish thy sad lonely lover.
(*sounds of shouting and fighting*)
What ruckus, and what noise is this today?

These are my friends, who make their wills the law
And chase some unhappy passenger. 15
They Love me well, yet I have much to do
To keep them from uncivil outrages.
Withdraw thee Valentine, who's this comes here?
Enter Proteus, Sylvia, and Julia disguised as Sebastian

PROTEUS
Madam, this service I have done for you,
Though you respect not what your servants do, 20
To hazard life, and rescue you from him
That would have forced your Honor, and your Love.
Give me for my gallant efforts, just one fair look,
A smaller prize then this I cannot beg,
And less than this, I am sure you cannot give. 25

VALENTINE (*aside*)
How like a dream is this? I see, and hear!
Love, lend me the patience to listen awhile.

SYLVIA
O miserable how unhappy I am.

PROTEUS
Unhappy were you, Madam, ere I came.
But by my coming, I have made you happy. 30

SYLVIA
By thy approach thou makes me most unhappy!

JULIA (*aside*)
And me, when he follows you everywhere.

SYLVIA
Had I been seized by a hungry Lion,
I would have been a breakfast to the Beast
Rather than have false Proteus rescue me. 35
Oh heaven be judge how I Love Valentine,
Whose life's as tender to me as my soul,

88

I do detest false perjured Proteus.
Therefore be gone, chase me no more.
PROTEUS
What dangerous action, stood it next to death   40
Would I not undergo, for one calm look,
Oh 'tis the curse in Love, and still approved
When women cannot Love, where they're beloved.
SYLVIA
When Proteus cannot Love, where he's beloved,
Read over Julia's heart, your first best Love   45
For whose dear sake, you did then split your faith
Into a thousand oaths, and all those oaths
Descended into perjury, to Love me.
You have no Love left now, unless you are two,
And that's far worse than none, better have none   50
Than broken Love, which is too much for one.
You abandoned and betrayed your true Friend!
PROTEUS
In Love,
Who respects friends?
SYLVIA
All men but Proteus.   55
PROTEUS
No, if the gentle spirit of flattering words,
Can no way change you to a milder form,
I'll woo you like a soldier, in a fight,
And Love you against the nature of Love, force you!
Proteus grabs Sylvia
Sylvia struggles and screams
PROTEUS
I'll force you to enjoy my desire.   60

VALENTINE

Barbarian! Stop that rude uncivil touch,

You Friend of an ill fashion!

PROTEUS

Valentine.

Sylvia stops struggling but Proteus does not let her go

VALENTINE

Thou evil child, that's without faith or Love,

Thou hast mislead my hopes. Only my own eyes   65

Could have persuaded me.

Who should be trusted, when one's right hand

Is perjured? Proteus

I am sorry I must never trust thee more,

But count the world a stranger for thy sake.   70

The private pain is deepest, oh time, most cursed,

Amongst all foes that a Friend should be the worst?

PROTEUS

My shame destroys me. Please

Forgive me Valentine, if my worst sorrow

Be sufficient penance for offense,   75

I suffered here. Thoughts and Prayers!

Regrets, for all I did commit.

VALENTINE

Oh Proteus. I forgive you.

Who by repentance is not satisfied?

And that my Love may appear plain and free,   80

All Sylvia's love I give up to thee.

Sylvia struggles again

JULIA (*aside*)

Oh, most unhappy!

Julia grabs her heart, fakes a heart attack, and dramatically falls

PROTEUS

Look to the gentle child.

VALENTINE

Why, gentle? Why wag? How now?

What's the matter? Look up! Speak!   85

JULIA

O good sir, my Master charged me to deliver a ring to Madam

Sylvia, which out of my neglect was never done.

PROTEUS

Where is that ring?

JULIA

Here 'tis, this is it.

Julia rises and hands Proteus a ring

PROTEUS

How? Let me see.   90

Why this is the ring I gave to Julia.

JULIA

Oh, cry you mercy sir, I have mistook.

This is the ring you sent to Sylvia.

Julia offers Proteus another ring

PROTEUS

How did you get this ring? At my farewell?

I gave this to Julia.   95

JULIA

And Julia herself did give it me,

And Julia herself hath brought it here.

Julia reveals herself

PROTEUS

How? Julia?

Proteus drops the limp Sylvia. Valentine scoops her up.

JULIA

Behold her, that was once the object of your affections,

And entertained them deeply in her heart. 100
Oh Proteus,
It is the lesser evil women finds,
For us to change our shapes, than men their minds.

PROTEUS

Then men their minds? 'Tis true, oh heaven, were man
But constant, he were perfect. That one error 105
Fills him with faults, makes him commit all the sins,
Inconstancy falls off where it begins.
What is in Sylvia's face, but I may spy
More fresh in Julia's, with a constant eye?

VALENTINE

Come, come, a hand from either. 110
Let me be blessed to make this happy close!
'Twere pity two such friends should be long foes.

PROTEUS

Bear witness, heaven, I have my wish forever!

JULIA

And I mine.

Julia falls into Proteus's arms. The men fist bump.
Enter Duke, Thurio, and Outlaws.

OUTLAW

A prize! A prize! A prize! 115

VALENTINE

Quiet, quiet I say. It is my Lord, the Duke.
(*Outlaws release Duke and Thurio*)
Your Grace is welcome to a man disgraced,
Banished Valentine.

DUKE

Sir Valentine?

THURIO

Yonder is Sylvia! And Sylvia's mine! 120

VALENTINE

    Thurio, stay back, or else embrace thy death.

    Come not within the length of my fists.

    Do not name Sylvia thine, if once again,

    Milan shall not hold you. Here she stands,

    Take but possession of her with a Touch,   125

    I dare you, but to breathe upon my Love!

THURIO

    Sir Valentine, I don't care for her, I don't.

    I hold him but a fool that will endanger

    His body, for a girl who loves him not!

    I claim her not, and so she is all yours.   130

DUKE

    The more degenerate and base you are

    To make such means for her, as you have done,

    And give her up so easily without a fight!

    Now, by the Honor of my Ancestry,

    I do applaud your spirit, Valentine,   135

    And think you worthy of an Empress's Love.

    Know then, I here forgive all former griefs,

    Cancel all grudge, welcome you home again,

    Hope you enjoy your future as I did,

    I see so much of me, Sir Valentine,   140

    You are a Gentleman, and well derived,

    Take your Sylvia, for you have earned her.

VALENTINE

    I thank your Grace, the gift has made me happy!

    I now beseech you, for your daughter's sake,

    To grant one favor that I shall ask of you   145

DUKE

    I grant it just for you, whatever it be.

VALENTINE

These banished men, that I have kept company,
Are men endowed with worthy qualities.
Forgive them what they have committed here,
And let them be recalled from their Exile.   150
They are reformed, civil, full of good,
And fit for great employment, worthy Lord.

DUKE

You have prevailed, I pardon them and you.
Employ them, as only you know best.
Come, away, we will celebrate all men,   155
With triumphs, mirth, and rare solemnity.

VALENTINE

And as we walk along, I dare be bold
To entertain your grace,
(*pointing to Julia*) See that young man?
What do you think?   160

DUKE

I think the youth has grace in him, he blushes.

VALENTINE

More grace than Boy, perhaps?

DUKE

What mean you by that?

VALENTINE

If it pleases you, I'll whisper on the way,
A silly tale, of women and dress ups!   165
Come Proteus, 'Tis a joy to watch you blush,
At the story of your Loves discovered.
That done, my day of marriage shall be yours,
One fate, one house, one mutual happiness.

Valentine and Proteus grin at each other

Exit

END OF PLAY